P9-DXN-704

THE BEAUTIFUL ONES

PRINCE

THE BEAUTIFUL ONES

Edited by Dan Piepenbring

WITHDRAWN

SPI
EGE
L&G
RAU

NEW YORK

Copyright © 2019 by NPG Music Publishing LLC

All rights reserved.

Published in the United States by Spiegel & Grau,
an imprint of Random House, a division
of Penguin Random House LLC, New York.

Spiegel & Grau and colophon are registered
trademarks of Penguin Random House LLC.

Text and photo credits are located on pages 278–79.

Hardback ISBN 9780399589652
Ebook ISBN 9780399589669

Printed in Germany on acid-free paper

randomhousebooks.com

246897531

First Edition

Designed by Triboro

THE
BEAUTIFUL
ONES

INTRO-
DUCTION

I LAST SPOKE TO PRINCE

on Sunday, April 17, 2016, four days before he died. That night I was lying in bed when my phone shuddered and lit up with a 952 area code. He'd never called my cell before, but I knew at once it was him. I scrambled for a pen and paper and plugged my phone into the wall—my battery was almost depleted. But my charging cord was only a foot long, so I couldn't stand up when I used the phone. I spent our final conversation hunched in the corner of my bedroom, taking notes by pressing the paper to the floor.

"Hi, Dan," he said, "it's Prince." Much has been written about Prince's speaking voice—the strange whispery fullness of it, reedy but low. Nowhere was this paradox more apparent than in that simple introduction: "Hi, Dan, it's Prince." He always used it. "I wanted to say that I'm alright," he said, "despite what the press would have you believe. They have to exaggerate everything, you know."

I had some idea. In the month since Prince had announced that "my brother Dan" was helping him work on his memoir, I'd seen it reported that I—twenty-eight years his junior, and white—was literally his brother. But the news now was of another order of magnitude. A few days earlier, Prince's plane had made an emergency landing after departing Atlanta, where he'd just finished what would be his final performance, part of a searching, contemplative solo tour he called "Piano & A Microphone." He'd been hospitalized in Moline, Illinois, supposedly to treat a resilient case of the flu.

Within hours of the story breaking on TMZ, Prince had tweeted from Paisley Park, in Chanhassen, Minnesota, saying that he was listening to his song "Controversy"—which begins, "I just can't believe all the things people say." Subtext: He was fine. Some residents of Chanhassen had seen him riding his bicycle. And the night before he called me, he'd thrown a dance party on his private soundstage, using the opportunity to show off a new purple guitar and a purple piano. "Wait a few days before you waste any prayers," he'd told the crowd.

"I was worried, but I saw on Twitter that you were okay," I told him. "I was sorry to hear you had the flu."

"I had flu-like symptoms," he said—a clarification that I'd dwell on a lot in the months to come. "And my voice was raspy." It still sounded that way to me, as if he was recovering from a severe cold. But he didn't want to linger on the subject. He'd called to talk about the book.

"I wanted to ask: Do you believe in cellular memory?" He was speaking of the idea that our bodies inherit our parents' memories—that experience is hereditary. "I was thinking about it because of reading the Bible," he explained. "The sins of the father. How is that possible without cellular memory?"

The concept resonated in his own life, too. "My father had two families. I was his second, and he wanted to do better with me than with his first son. So he was very orderly, but my mother didn't like that. She liked spontaneity and excitement."

Prince wanted to explain how he emerged as the synthesis of his parents. Their conflict lived within him. In their discord, he heard a strange harmony that inspired him to create. He was full of awe and insight about his mother and father, about the way he embodied their union and disunion.

"One of my life's dilemmas has been looking at this," he told me as I sat on my floor, scribbling away. "I like order, finality, and truth. But if I'm out at a fancy dinner party or something, and the DJ puts on something funky . . ."

"You'll have to dance," I said.

"Right. Like, listen to this." He held the phone up to a studio monitor and played a few bars of something that sounded boisterous, brassy, and earthy, like a house party from many decades ago. "It's funky, right? That's from Judith Hill's new album. It's the first time I'm hearing it."

He paused for a moment. "We need to find a word," he said, "for what funk is."

THE
QUEST
FOR
THAT
WORD

was never far from Prince's mind in those days. His asides to the crowds at his Piano & A Microphone shows often found him reflecting on the rudiments of funk. "The space in between the notes—that's the good part," he would say. "However long the space is—that's how funky it is. Or how funky it ain't." Unpacking these ideas is part of what made him want to write a book in the first place.

Though Prince had published several photo books, and though he'd entertained the notion of something more substantial at various points in his career, the genesis of this project came in late 2014, when his manager and attorney, Phaedra Ellis-Lamkins, sought out a literary agent to represent him. Prince chose Esther Newberg, of the talent agency ICM Partners. She represented his friend Harry Belafonte, and he liked her old-school sensibility—plus, she appealed to him as a matriarch in a patriarchal industry. By early 2015, Prince had

6

signed off on a concept, a book of lyrics with his own introduction and annotations. Newberg and her colleague Dan Kirschen shopped the idea to eager publishers, but Prince's camp never finalized a deal, and for most of 2015 he focused on music.

In mid-November, he turned to the book with renewed enthusiasm. "He would like to fast-track a project," Ellis-Lamkins wrote to Newberg. Working with Trevor Guy, an aide who helped with business affairs, Prince, Esther, and Dan expanded the book's nebulous purview. What if it included not just annotated lyrics but unpublished sketches, photos, and ephemera? The word *memoir* wasn't part of the conversation yet, but Prince wanted to begin work on the project right away. Trevor suggested convening a group of editors at Paisley Park to discuss it in person.

The book coincided with an inward turn in Prince's music-making. Having traveled the world in recent years with his electrifying band 3RDEYEGIRL, he was electing to play alone now. He envisioned a tour comprising just him and his piano. The intimate, amorphous sets would span his career without the constraints and pyrotechnics of an arena show. Hosting a group of European journalists at Paisley Park, he explained that he relished the thrill of taking the stage unadorned, paring his songs down to their essential components and reinventing them on the fly. He'd been practicing into the night, playing alone for hours on end, his piano filling the vast darkness of his soundstage until he found something that he described as "transcendence." This was what he wanted to share.

He'd booked dates across Europe when terrorists in Paris attacked the Bataclan, a concert hall he'd played three times. The violence, combined with price gouging by ticket resellers, convinced him to scuttle the tour. Why not just host the shows at Paisley Park? On his home turf, he could mount a production befitting the price.

As Prince's vision for Piano & A Microphone found clarity, his book began to take shape, too. According to one friend, several of the people he loved and admired were falling ill, making him conscious of his own mortality. More than ever, he saw the value in telling his own story. On January 11, 2016, a few weeks before he gave his first solo performance, he invited three editors to meet with him at Paisley Park, where he'd explain his ambitions and decide which publishing house he wanted to work with. A meeting with multiple competing editors at the same time was an atypical arrangement. And then there were all the rumors they'd heard: Didn't he bristle at questions about his past? Would he eject anyone who used profanity, or demand a contribution to his swear jar? Was it true you weren't allowed to look him in the eye?

As soon as Prince walked into the meeting, any sense of trepidation dissolved. He was charming, engaged, even self-deprecating. ("I ramble sometimes," he said.) For the next two hours, he presided over a freewheeling discussion of his past, his musical philosophy, and his aspirations for the book. He wanted to write a memoir, he declared—a decision he'd arrived at so recently that even Trevor, who sat in on the meeting, was surprised by it. It would be called *The Beautiful Ones,* after one of the most naked, aching songs in his catalog.

The story would focus on his mother, whose gaze was "the first I ever saw," and who had never received proper credit for her role in his success. He shared an assortment of objects with the assembled editors. He'd asked his sister Tyka to send him old family photos, including many of his parents, and a family tree. He'd also tracked down the original cover art for *1999,* a collage ornamented with cutouts of a phone booth, a futuristic skyline, and a nude woman with a horse's head. And he presented the first iteration of a screenplay, *Dreams,* that would become *Purple Rain.*

One of the editors asked Prince about songwriting. It was fundamentally aspirational, he thought. You write where you want to go. From his earliest memories, he told the group, he wrote music to imagine—and reimagine—himself. Being an artist was a constant evolution, not to mention a form of symbiosis with whoever or whatever surrounded you when you made music. He'd created a persona almost as a prophetic act: He could become the person he imagined. His whole life was an act of imagining, creating, and becoming. Today having a persona is considered more or less essential to superstardom; for Prince, it was inseparable from his identity as an artist.

Early on, he'd recognized the inherent mystery of this process, and the power of preserving that mystery, or even further obscuring it.

"Mystery is a word for a reason," he said. "It has a purpose." The right book could add new layers to his mystery, Prince thought, even as it stripped others away. It would have to function as his autobiography, but in a form that was sui generis, as capacious and shape-shifting as its author. Never one to shrink from grand promises, he offered only one formal guideline: It had to be the biggest music book of all time.

The meeting had no official conclusion. At some point, after cracking a joke, Prince just got up and left, carrying himself out on peals of his own laughter. He slipped into the room about ten minutes later with not a word about his absence. Then he said it was time for dinner, and disappeared again. The editors got excited—dinner with Prince!—before they realized they weren't invited, and he wasn't coming back.

SOON AFTER THAT MEETING

Prince put on his first ever Piano & A Microphone show at Paisley Park, executing the ideas he'd laid out a few months before. The show wove storytelling and reflection into songs that stretched from his first record, *For You,* to his most current, *HITnRUN Phase Two.* His spoken contributions gave an idea of what was on his mind at the time. He was processing his past. Only when I saw the footage more than a year later did I see how this performance dovetailed with his ideas for *The Beautiful Ones.*

As soon as he sat down at his piano that evening, Prince began a kind of stream-of-consciousness regression. Suddenly he was a kid again, sharing his earliest musical memories. "I wish I could play piano," he told the crowd in this childlike mode. "But I don't know how to play piano. Everything looks different. Three years old—the piano looks bigger at three years old. Mmm . . . Maybe I'll just watch TV." He leaped onto his piano and pantomimed eating popcorn in front of the television.

"Here comes Dad. Not supposed to touch it, and I wanna play it so bad. . . . There goes Dad. Him and Mom are getting divorced now." Then he added the second person to the mix, as if his father were in the room. "I'm actually happy to see you go. . . . I was only seven years old. But now: I can play piano anytime I want." Prince pounded out a few bars from the original theme to *Batman.*

"Can't play the piano like Dad, though," he said. "How does Dad do that? Let me see . . . I wish I could sing." He added: "I thought I would never be able to play like my dad, and he never missed an opportunity to remind me of that. But we got along good. He was my best friend." They used to take turns playing Ray Charles's "Unchain My Heart."

Before this show, it would've been hard to imagine Prince uttering anything so forthright onstage. That night's set included "Sometimes I Feel Like a Motherless Child," a traditional spiritual that was also, in its way, an expression of longing for the vanished world of his parents. He was "a long way from home," he sang. "Sometimes I feel like I'm almost gone."

Maybe the barest assertion of melancholy came later in the evening. "How many of you have lucid dreams?" he asked the crowd. "I like dreaming now more than I used to. Some of my friends have passed away, and I see them in my dreams. It's like they're here, and the dreams are just like waking sometimes."

There's something about these lines, some combination of restful and restive, that makes me sad now. It's easy to put too much weight on these things in hindsight, but they strike me as the thoughts of a man half in love with easeful Death, to borrow a phrase. Then he sang the first line of "Sometimes It Snows in April," itself one of the most plangent songs in his catalog. "Tracy died soon after a long-fought civil war . . ."

WITHIN DAYS OF

this—his first ever solo show, and arguably the most emotionally direct of his career—Prince chose an editor for his memoir: Chris Jackson of Spiegel & Grau, an imprint of Random House. He liked that Chris had worked on Jay-Z's book, *Decoded*. Not wanting to lose momentum, he enlisted Chris, Trevor, and ICM's Esther and Dan to help him find a cowriter. His former manager Julia Ramadan had once told him, "When it comes to your life story, don't let anyone else hold the pen." Now, it seemed, he was preparing to do just that. No one, maybe not even Prince himself, was certain of how the process would work.

This is when I got involved. Dan Kirschen, my agent, had known for years of my admiration for Prince. He'd seen the poster in my bedroom; he'd watched me sing "Kiss" at a karaoke bar; he'd let me show him clips from the *Sign o' the Times* concert film. Even so, when he told me that he'd found himself in the happy position of seeking Prince's cowriter, I don't think he was prepared for how abjectly I would beg to be in the running. He agreed to put me on the list, but he didn't mince words: The likelihood of my getting the gig fell somewhere between winning the lottery and surviving an asteroid impact. For one thing, I'd published zero books. At the time, I was an editor at *The Paris Review,* a literary magazine that I didn't know if Prince had read or even heard of—no doubt his worst-selling album had found a wider audience than the *Review* ever had. I was twenty-nine. Next to the more seasoned hands up for the job, many of whom had loved Prince for longer than I'd been alive, I was a guaranteed also-ran.

But when ICM and Random House floated several high-profile candidates, Prince demurred. He was in the habit of reading reviews of his shows from nonprofessionals, especially the rhapsodic write-ups that fans tweeted or posted on their blogs. These were the people he felt deserved the job. As untested as they were, he'd inspired them to write, and they might inspire him, too.

As one aide later recalled, Prince looked at the writing process through the prism of music: He wanted an improvisational partner, someone he could open up to and with whom he could arrange his story like a song or an album. As long as the rapport was there, he'd sooner take on a dedicated novice than a veteran. Of course, publishers would balk at the idea of hiring some teenage Prince fanatic whose sole résumé item was a self-published concert review. In the spirit of compromise, he returned the list of potential cowriters and eliminated all but two names, mine being one of them. We were the only ones who'd never published books.

Dan told me that Prince was now in possession of my phone number. I should expect a call anytime, day or night. I started to sleep with my phone beside my pillow, the ringer set ear-piercingly high. And I practiced my greeting, ironing out any traces of exclamation that crept into my voice. My aim was to sound as nonchalant as possible. "Hi, Prince." "Hello, Prince." "Ah, is this Prince? Hey. Good to hear from you."

But the call never came. Instead, Trevor devised an assignment. We potential collaborators were to submit personal statements to Prince about our relationship to his music, and why we thought we could do the job. I submitted my statement at 8:30 that same night.

To call it heavy on flattery would be an understatement. There are parts of it I'd write differently today if I had the chance. Certainly I never intended it for anyone's eyes but his. Here's some of what I wrote:

When I listen to Prince, I feel like I'm breaking the law. . . . My first time driving alone in Baltimore, I switched on the radio and heard a man singing about wanting to be a woman, baring this raw, psychosexual wish to understand his girlfriend better—and it blew the hinges off the door in my head. "For you naked I would dance a ballet." It was the most sensitive, singular, honest, *dangerous* piece of music I'd ever heard. I half expected to get pulled over if anyone caught me listening to it so closely. . . .

If Prince wants to write a book, I want to help him write it: to put his voice on the page. . . . I'd see the project as an extension of the songwriting—not as a kind of journalism or interview, but a chance to find a new way of connecting with his audience, and beyond. People might ask, Isn't he too elusive to get on paper? There's this idea that nonfiction destroys the mystery of the author—but when it's done well, it only deepens that mystery. From my first encounter with Prince, over the air-waves in Baltimore, I knew he was a master storyteller, an ecstatic, transcendent original: To help him tell his stories in a new mode would be a once-in-a-lifetime honor.

Trevor's response came less than twelve hours later, at 2:23 in the morning. "Is Dan Piepenbring available to meet with PRN at Paisley Park on Friday evening (tomorrow)?" he wrote to Dan and Esther.

Dan, who was used to Paisley communiques arriving at ungodly hours, read the note promptly and paced his apartment until the sun came up. Then he kept calling me until I woke up. I whooped. He whooped. The next morning, January 29, I was on a plane to Minneapolis.

IN A 1996 INTERVIEW WITH OPRAH,

Prince explained why he stayed in Minnesota when most of his peers favored life on the coasts: "It's so cold, it keeps the bad people out." Sure enough, there was an entrenched layer of snow on the ground when I landed, and it wasn't just the bad people who were away—hardly anyone seemed to be around at all.

Prince's driver, Kim Pratt, picked me up at the airport in a big black Escalade, wearing a plastic diamond the size of a Ring Pop. "Sometimes you gotta femme it up," she said.

My meeting at Paisley Park was still hours away—no one seemed to know when, exactly—so Kim dropped me off at the Country Inn & Suites, an unremarkable chain hotel in Chanhassen that served as a de facto Paisley substation. One of Prince's aides told me he'd lived there for so many years that he'd broken the recumbent bicycle in the hotel's fitness center. Apparently Prince had paid for enough rooms there to have bought the place four times over.

I was "on call" until further notice. I felt like I was joining a long and august line of people who'd been made to wait by Prince, people who had sat in rooms in this same hotel, maybe in this very room, quietly freaking out just as I was quietly freaking out. I turned the television on. I turned the television off. I had a mint tea. My room looked out onto sun-bleached shingles, a pine tree, and a disused ladder. Since I knew photography was strictly verboten at Paisley, I took a picture of this view instead.

Around 6:30, Kim texted to let me know she was picking me up. P—everyone in the Paisleysphere called him "P," I would discover—was ready to see me.

The sun had set, so my first glimpse of Paisley came under cover of darkness. From the outside, it's disconcertingly unassuming. It was illuminated by purple sconces when Kim drove up to it, but even so, I would've believed that it was the regional headquarters of a defense contractor, or a showroom for coextruded plastic products. There was almost nothing around it—I had never fully appreciated how isolated it was. I confessed to Kim that I was nervous, that my heart was racing. She laughed it off.

"You'll be fine," she said as she parked in front of the complex.

My right hand was freezing. Mindful of the fact that Prince might soon be shaking it, I sat on it to warm it up.

"He's really sweet. You'll see," Kim said. "Actually, looks like you'll see now—that's him at the door."

And so it was. Prince was standing alone at the front door to Paisley Park ready to introduce himself.

"Dan. Nice to meet you. I'm Prince." His voice was full of calm, and lower than I'd expected.

In the foyer, the lights were dim, and though preparations for the night's concert were underway not a hundred feet from us—Judith Hill was playing in a few hours on the Paisley soundstage, followed by Morris Day and the Time—this part of the complex was empty. The silence was broken only by cooing doves, live ones, in a cage on the second floor. Scented candles flickered from the corners; their sweetness dominated the room. Prince was wearing a loose draped top in a marled sienna, with matching pants, a green vest, and a pair of beaded necklaces. His afro was concealed beneath an olive-green beanie. The sneakers he favored in his final years, white platforms with light-up Lucite soles, flashed red as he led me up a short flight of stairs and across a small skyway to a conference room.

"Are you hungry?" he asked.

"No, I'm okay," I said, though I hadn't eaten since morning.

"Too bad," Prince said. "I'm starving."

I winced. We'd exchanged fewer than a dozen words and already we were out of alignment.

In the conference room, his trademark glyph was etched into a long glass table. Toward the back, a heart-shaped couch sat beside a fern. On the vaulted ceiling, a mural depicted a purple nebula bordered by piano keys. Prince sat at the head of the table and told me to take the seat next to him—a bit of instruction he always offered, I'd later notice. "Sit here." He gave the impression of someone who'd grown accustomed to choreographing the space around him.

"Smells good in here," I said.

"Yeah, I like candles," Prince said.

First things first: Had I brought a copy of my statement? He wanted to go over it together. I hadn't, but I could read it from my phone, if he wanted. I fumbled for it in my pocket, fearing that I was already in over my head. I knew Prince did not suffer phones gladly. Mine had a cracked screen, which I hoped would endear me to him. I cleared my throat and began: "When I listen to Prince, I feel like I'm breaking the law."

"Now, let me stop you right there," Prince said. "Why did you write that?"

It dawned on me that he might have flown me all the way out to Minneapolis just to tell me that I knew nothing of his work.

"The music I make isn't breaking the law, to me," he said. "I write in harmony. I've always lived in harmony—like this." He gestured at the room. "The candles." He asked if I'd heard of the devil's interval, or the tritone: a combination of notes that created a brooding, menacing dissonance. It reminded him of Led Zeppelin. Their kind of rock music, bluesy and harsh, broke the rules of harmony. Robert Plant's keening voice—*that* sounded law-breaking to him as a kid. Not any of the music that he and his friends made. Prince was serious about this, even grave. I tried to make a joke about how some songs might qualify as misdemeanors while others were capital crimes. He remained stone-faced.

Okay. We were off to a frosty start. Behind his sphinxlike features, I could sense his skepticism about me. I tried to calm

14

my nerves by making as much eye contact as possible. Though his face was unlined and his skin glowing, his eyes betrayed trace elements of fatigue. It came and went, but it was there: a glassiness, a fleeting restlessness.

I kept reading my statement. To my relief, much of it sat better with him than the first lines had. We spoke a lot about diction. Prince had developed fastidious ideas about which words belonged in his orbit and which did not. "Certain words don't describe me," he said. There were terms bandied about in the white critical establishment that demonstrated a complete lack of awareness of who he was. Actually, all the books about him were wrong because they embraced these white critical terms. *Alchemy* was one. When writers ascribed alchemical qualities to his music, they were ignoring the literal meaning of the word, the dark art of turning metal into gold. He would never do something like that. His object was harmony.

He reserved a special ire for the word *magical.* I'd used some version of it in my statement.

"Funk is the opposite of magic," he said. "Funk is about rules." It was human, the result of work and sweat—there was nothing magical about it.

He said he liked "some of the stuff" I wrote about him: about his origins, correcting the record, finding a voice, preserving the mystery. Now he was curious about the process. What did writing a book have in common with writing an album? I could tell that he wanted to learn: to apply the same diligence with craft and technique that he'd used to master so many different instruments. He wanted to know the rules, so he could know if and when to flout them.

Here our conversation, which lasted about ninety minutes, opened up a bit, and we both started to enjoy ourselves more. Talks with Prince, I was learning, were discursive affairs. Subjects would rise to the surface, submerge a minute or two later, and come bubbling back up five minutes after that. Invariably we touched on a handful of the same topics: God, love, race in America, the duplicity of the music industry, and the elusive nature of creativity, technology, and the past.

He said he was finished with making music, making records. "I'm sick of playing the guitar, at least for now. I like the piano, but I hate the thought of picking up the guitar." What he really wanted to do was write. "I want to write lots of books. It's all up here," he said, pointing to his temple. That's why he wanted to talk to writers and to work with a publisher. "I want my first book to be better than my first album. I like my first album, but . . ." he trailed off. "I'm a lot smarter than I was then."

In fact, he was so bursting with ideas for his first book that he didn't know where to begin. Maybe he wanted to focus on scenes from his early life, juxtaposed against moments set in the present day. Or maybe he wanted to do a whole book on the inner workings of the music industry. Or maybe he should write mainly about his mother: He'd been wanting to articulate her role in his life.

Then there was the matter of tone. He had a skillful comic voice, and he gravitated toward comedy. At the same time, he didn't want something too frothy. The book would have to surprise people—provoke them, motivate them. Ideally it would become a form of cultural currency. "I want something that's passed around from friend to friend, like—do you know *Waking Life*?" Richard Linklater's surreal 2001 movie—I said I did. "You don't show that to all your friends, just the ones who can hang." Books like Miles Davis's autobiography, or John Howard Griffin's *Black Like Me,* were natural touchstones, he thought.

First and foremost, the book would allow him to seize the narrative of his own life. Once, he said, he'd seen a former employee of his on TV saying she thought it was her God-given duty to preserve and protect the unreleased material in his vault. "Now, that sounds like someone I should call the police on," he told me. "How is that not racist?" People were always casting him—and all black artists—in a helpless role, he said, as if he were incapable of managing himself. "I still have to brush my own teeth."

Similarly, he wanted to combat the notion that he was some "egotistical maniac," someone who got off on withholding the pleasures of his catalog from the undeserving masses. Take "Extraloveable," for instance—a song that had finally appeared in 2011, though bootlegs had been making the rounds since the eighties. "It wasn't released in the eighties because it wasn't done. If any track is unreleased, it's because it's not done."

If his story were properly told, he could exist in a new musical context. He mentioned a writer who'd compared him to Bruce Springsteen. "Why? No one has any of his albums here. No one listens to him. I don't. You might as well compare me to Billy Joel. Why aren't they comparing me to Sly Stone?" It went the other way, too. Every week, music journalists were comparing a new musician to him. "When they don't write, produce, play every track—not many young players have the technical skill." It bespoke a lack of imagination, a diminished range. Musicians now could only be like so many other musicians; the press wouldn't reach for anything too obscure. Prince recalled Santana, and the unique marketing of that band in the late sixties and seventies—the way they dressed, their songwriting. "I don't see anything like that these days. And why aren't I compared to Santana?"

To his mind, the dismal state of music could be blamed on Apple, who'd cornered a distribution model that devalued artists; and on record labels, which had locked themselves into an outmoded way of doing business. He wanted to devote a chapter to both of them, to how out of touch record executives could be. Not long ago, for a friend, he'd played a song by Betty Davis, a funk singer who'd been briefly married to Miles Davis. Though the friend was very knowledgeable, he'd never heard of her. "That's a good example of music in neglect, because labels are letting it rot, not knowing how to distribute it or keep it alive." You could see the problem just by looking at Jimmy Iovine's house, he said. Iovine, an industry mogul and one of its highest earners, "has a guy whose job it is to control all his remotes. Keep them with fresh batteries, make sure they all work." Prince imitated him: " 'Hey, you should come out to my house!' Yeah, right. . . ."

He noticed my phone still sitting on the conference room table, and his trust seemed to falter for a moment. "That thing's not on, is it?"

"No," I said, sweeping it off the table. And it wasn't. Though he never made it explicit, I didn't try to record him or take notes. (As soon as I got back to my hotel room, I retraced as much of our conversation as possible; I've used quotation marks only in cases of high confidence that I've captured his remarks verbatim.)

As our conversation turned again toward chains of distribution and questions of ownership, I saw that Prince's dispute with Warner Bros. remained one of the central traumas of his life, a lens through which he understood questions of race, property, and creativity. With the help of his lawyer, Ellis-Lamkins, he'd recently repossessed his master recordings from Warner Bros., a victory that marked the beginning of the most liberated phase of his life. All artists should own their masters, he said, especially black artists. He saw it as a way to fight racism. Black communities would restore wealth by amassing their master recordings. And they would protect that wealth, hiring their own police, founding their own schools, and forming bonds on their own terms.

The music industry had siloed black music from the start, he reminded me. They'd promote black artists for the "black base," and then, if they captured that base, they would try to "cross over." Billboard had developed totally unnecessary charts to measure and quantify this division, and it continued to this day, even if the "black charts" now masqueraded under euphemisms like "R&B/Hip-Hop."

"Why didn't Warner Bros. ever think I could be president of the label?" It never occurred to them that he could run his own operation. "I want to say in a meeting with big record executives,

'Okay, you're racist.' How would you feel if I said that to you?"
He settled his eyes on mine with a blazing intensity that arose,
I noticed, whenever he started to talk about the recording in-
dustry's treatment of black artists.

"Can we write a book that solves racism?" he asked.

Before I could say yes, or at least "we could try," he broke in
with another question: "What do you think racism means?" This
was one of Prince's rhetorical talents—a sudden, unprompted
directness that forced you to address questions usually considered too lofty for casual conversation. I remember thinking
what a refreshingly plainspoken question it was. Then I realized
I had to answer it.

After sputtering for a few seconds, I offered something like the
dictionary definition of racism: discrimination and oppression
based on the idea that someone's race was inferior—plus all
the structural, systemic, institutionalized versions of the same.
I don't know what he thought of that; he only nodded slightly.
It may have been technically correct, but it was gutless, the
kind of studious, safe response that might fly at a job interview
with anyone other than Prince. He could've gotten a similar
answer from Siri. If our book was going to solve racism, de-
scribing it clinically wouldn't do the trick.

Prince shared some of his earliest memories of racism in
Minneapolis. His best friend growing up was Jewish. "He
looked a lot like you," he said. One day someone threw a stone
at the boy—the first racist act that Prince could recall having
witnessed. North Minneapolis was a black community, so it
wasn't until a bit later, when he and others in his neighborhood were bused to a predominantly white elementary school,
that Prince felt racism firsthand. In retrospect, he believed that
Minnesota in the era of busing was no more enlightened than
segregationist Alabama; he'd sung scathingly about the experience on 1992's "The Sacrifice of Victor."

"I went to school with the rich kids," he told me, "who didn't
like having me there." When one of them called him the N-
word, Prince threw a punch. "I felt I had to. Luckily the guy ran
away crying. But if there was a fight—where would it end?
Where should it end? How do you know when to fight?"

Those questions became all the more tangled as racism took
on insidious shapes and hidden guises. "I mean, All Lives Matter,
you understand the irony in that," he said, referring to an anti–
Black Lives Matter slogan that was finding some traction at the
moment. I agreed; it missed the point entirely.

"I'll be honest, I don't think you could write the book," Prince
told me at one point. He thought I needed to know more about
racism—to have felt it. And going back to diction, he talked
about hip-hop and the way it transformed words. It takes white

18

language—"your language"—and makes it something white people can't understand. Miles Davis, he reminded me, believed in only two categories of thinking: the truth, and white bullshit.

And yet, a little later on, when we were discussing the music industry's many forms of dominion over artists, I said something that galvanized him. I wondered what his interest in publishing a book was, given that the music business had modeled itself on book publishing. Contracts, advances, royalties, revenue splits, copyrights: Much of the ingrained approach to intellectual property that he abhorred in record labels had its origins with book publishers. His face lit up. "I can see myself typing that," he said, pantomiming a keyboard. "'You may be wondering why I'm working with . . .'"

All of this stands to address a question I've heard a lot since that day: Why did Prince choose me? I don't know. I'll never know. There was never a moment when he told me in clear terms why he felt we should work together. At the end of that first conversation, I still didn't know where I stood with him. My sense is that what started as a stiff exchange had evolved into something agreeably sinuous, the kind of talk you can imagine continuing long into the night, touching glancingly on any number of themes. It was an interview in the purest sense of the word, an exchange of ideas. We'd been speaking for well over an hour when he paused for a moment.

"Do you know what time it is?" he asked.

By that point, we were in such a rarefied place that I assumed he was asking some kind of rhetorical question. No: He wanted to know literally what time it was. I checked my phone and told him. That night's concert was soon to be underway on the soundstage—it was time to wrap up our meeting. He disappeared for a moment to call his driver, who was, apparently, already engaged.

"It's okay," he said when he came back. "I'll take you myself."

I followed him out of the conference room and into an elevator where, less than three months later, he would be found dead. It was an impossible outcome to imagine. Vivacious, bouncing on the balls of his feet, he reiterated his wish to write many books as he punched the button for the bottom floor. "You got me hopped up on this industry talk," he said. "But I'm still thinking about writing on my mother."

The elevator opened into a dimly lit basement. I had barely enough time to notice the word *Vault* painted beside a nearby doorway before Prince led me out to the garage. He was walking briskly toward a black Lincoln MKT, but I noticed other cars and motorcycles, including a limousine and what appeared to be a golden Cadillac.

Climbing into the Lincoln's passenger seat, I noticed a fistful of loose twenty-dollar bills in the cupholder. Prince activated the garage door and we pulled out into Paisley's main lot, now noticeably fuller than it had been when I arrived. "Looks like people are starting to show up," he said, like a performer peeking from behind the curtain just before showtime. He sounded genuinely excited, as if the thrill of putting a concert together had lost none of its luster over time. There were a few people lingering in the lot, but none of them seemed to realize that it was Prince driving past them; no one was pointing or waving.

Turning out of Paisley, he picked up a good bit of speed and again indulged his fixation on chains of distribution: who controls a piece of intellectual property, and who makes money on it. "Tell Esther [Newberg, of ICM] and Random House that I want to own my book. That you and I would co-own it, take it to all the distribution channels." We didn't need them to interfere in the publication process any more than was necessary, he thought. We needed a process where the trust, responsibility, and accountability were all ours, jointly. "I'm not counting your money; you're not counting mine."

"No matter what you decide to do, if you ever want to talk about your ideas, I'm happy to serve as a sounding board," I said.

"I like your style," he told me. "Just look at a word and see if it's one I would use. Because *magic* isn't one I'd use. Magic is Michael's word," he said. (Michael was Michael Jackson, whom Prince only referred to by his first name.) "That's what his music was about."

That left me plenty of room for an obvious follow-up question: What *is* your music about, then? I didn't ask that question. I was more consumed by the moment-to-moment reality of occupying a motor vehicle with Prince in the driver's seat. His posture, for instance: upright. His turn signaling: impeccable. But wasn't this exactly the sort of gee-whiz exoticizing that he'd inveighed against a few minutes ago? He'd told me he brushed his own teeth every morning. Why shouldn't he have been an excellent driver? To believe that everything around him was glazed in surrealism was tantamount to believing in a kind of magic, too.

In the portico of the Country Inn, he put the car in park and we kept talking. "I've never seen race, in a certain way—I've tried to be nice to everyone," he said. He seemed to think that too few of his white contemporaries had the same evenhandedness, even as they feted him for it. DeRay McKesson, a Black Lives Matter activist, had recently appeared on Stephen Colbert's *Late Show* for an interview in which the host had traded places with the guest, inviting McKesson to sit in the interviewer's chair. "He's a guy who's trying to get it," Prince said of Colbert. "Letterman would've never done that. It's time for him to sit down. Time for a lot of people in the music business to sit down." When it came time to sell and promote this book, Prince wanted to deal only with the Colberts of the world, people who understood that his business practices, however unorthodox they might appear, were about empowerment and equality.

"There's a lot of people who say you gotta learn to walk before you learn to run. That's slave talk to me. That's something slaves would say."

With that, he thanked me for my time, offered me a firm handshake, and left me at the automatic doors to the Country Inn & Suites.

ABOUT AN HOUR LATER,

following a bout of frenetic note-taking punctuated by celebratory dancing and karate kicking, I was on my way back to Paisley. Prince's assistant Meron Bekure came to pick me up. And, inadvertently, she broadened my impression of his autonomy: Though she had booked my flight, she had no idea why I was there.

"So, you're a . . . journalist?" she asked. "You're here to do an interview?"

When I explained that Prince was intending to write a book, she seemed surprised. But we didn't have much time to sort it out—soon we were back at the Paisley lot, now loaded with cars. Meron led me in through a side entrance, past a security guard, and into a crush of revelers in the midst of enjoying Judith Hill's set. The soundstage was stupefyingly large, and I couldn't figure out how it connected to the part of the complex where I'd met Prince earlier—the true labyrinthine vastness of the place was only beginning to set in.

I saw no sign of Prince anywhere, but he must've seen me. A few minutes after I arrived, a large man in a paisley suit jacket tapped me on the shoulder. It was Kirk Johnson, Prince's friend and bodyguard and the Paisley Park facilities manager.

"Are you Dan?" he asked. "Prince would like you to join him in the VIP stand." Sure enough, there he was: draped inconspicuously across a couch on a riser toward the back of the room, dressed more elegantly than he'd been before. He indicated that I should take the seat beside him.

It was loud—Prince cupped my ear. "What do you think of the show so far?" He pointed to a guitarist. "That's Tony Maiden. Rufus's guitarist. I learned how to play rhythm guitar from him. I saw him earlier and gave him a big hug. It was like hugging your elementary school teacher."

Hill finished her set. Before long, Morris Day and the Time took the stage: loud suits, gilded mirror, and all.

"We're gonna play a slow song now," Day told the crowd, before they launched into "Girl." "I bet y'all didn't even know we *had* slow songs. See if you remember this one." Prince slid in close and cupped my ear again: "I think *I* do."

During "Ice Cream Castles," he wrinkled his face up as if he'd just heard a corny joke: "They're not even *trying* to sing."

Later, Day reminisced about "that yellow limousine—you know, the one from *Purple Rain*. I think it's in the basement here somewhere."

Prince slid over again to whisper, "It ain't."

And during "The Walk"—another song he wrote—Prince played what I can only describe as the most meticulous air bass I've ever seen. If someone had approached with an actual bass and slipped it into his hands, I'm confident it would've fit perfectly; he would've been hitting every note.

Between all this, he found the time to entertain the crowd and bring me a bottle of water. Toward the finale of their set, though, he skittered off the riser and disappeared without a farewell. As the crowd thinned, I realized he wasn't coming back—and that maybe my experience with him had drawn to a close. We'd had an excellent night, but I had no idea if I was getting the job or not. I also had no idea how I was getting back to the hotel. A group of women approached me with a folded note.

"Will you give this to him?"

I thought of how best to explain. "To be honest, I'm not sure I'll ever see him again."

They looked puzzled. "That's okay. We might not, either." One of them pressed the note into my hand: a short expression of their undying admiration, with names, email addresses, and phone numbers.

I went in search of Meron and was intercepted by Kirk, who came bearing a message of his own: "He said to tell you he had a good time talking and he'll call you soon." In exchange, I passed him the note I'd received from the women.

No sooner had Meron dropped me off at the Country Inn than she called to say that Prince wanted to call me *very* soon—in my hotel room, that night. By now it was 2:30 in the morning. "What's the room number?" she asked. I ran out to the hall to make sure I was getting it right: 255. When we hung up, I saw I'd left the door on the latch. In the time it took me to walk over and close it, I missed a call from her on my cell. "Did I miss something?" I texted. No answer. I stayed up till dawn, but Prince never called that night.

AROUND FOUR O'CLOCK

the next afternoon, having availed myself of one of Chanhassen's fine chain eateries, I was on the sidewalk outside the Country Inn when I saw him again: Prince, at the wheel of his Lincoln MKT, pulling out of the hotel lot, his afro looming disproportionately large in the driver's side window. I watched him idle at a traffic light in front of a bank, beside a dirty snowdrift. For some reason, sighting him in the wild felt even stranger than riding with him. What was he doing? Interviewing another writer, maybe, or running some leisurely weekend errands? Then I worried that he'd called my room, failed to reach me, and driven over to see where I'd gone.

When I got back to my room, I saw that Trevor had emailed a link from Prince: a short video on Facebook about the continuing relevance of the Doll Test, the famous experiment in which children, including black children, associated a white doll with goodness, kindness, and beauty, and a black doll with badness, cruelty, and ugliness. "Why is that doll ugly?" the researcher asked a black child in the video. "Because he's black," the child answered. The video was captioned: WE'RE DOING SOMETHING VERY WRONG.

I'd just reconciled myself to a Saturday night alone in Chanhassen when Meron texted with a change of plans. There was to be a dance party at Paisley, followed by a movie screening. She would pick me up.

The dance party, it turned out, was an employees-only affair: Meron, Trevor, two members of 3RDEYEGIRL, and two musicians from Prince's newest recording project, the bassist MonoNeon and the saxophonist Adrian Crutchfield. On a plinth surrounded by couches and candles was DJ Kiss, who'd helmed the turntables at last night's concert; she spun records for just the seven of us in a high-ceilinged room adjacent to the soundstage. An elaborate fruit plate had been set out. A mural of black jazz musicians from Prince's *Rainbow Children* era was on the wall; we stood on a huge black rug with *NPG Music Club* on it, sometimes tripping over one of the letters as it started to unpeel. A large silver ♀ symbol was suspended from the ceiling. On a stairway railing was the grille of an old car, the same one from the *Sign o' the Times* cover. And most impressively, two massive projection screens were broadcasting *Barbarella* on repeat. Twin versions of Jane Fonda, thirty feet tall, strutted around a foreign planet in formfitting futurewear.

There were whispers that Prince might join us that night on the dance floor, such as it was, but he never appeared. Instead, Meron slipped off to return holding a bundle of our coats, and announced that it was time for the movie.

"I thought this *was* the movie," I said, gesturing at one of the writhing Jane Fondas.

"Oh, no!" she said. "We're seeing *Kung Fu Panda 3*."

Apparently, Prince regularly arranged for private after-hours screenings at the nearby Chanhassen Cinema. We headed over in two cars and found a lone attendant in the empty parking lot ready to unlock the door.

Prince arrived just after the movie began, slipping into the back row.

"Meron," he asked, "is there popcorn?" She went out to fetch some. We watched as the animated panda ate many dumplings and relegated evildoers to the Spirit Realm. I heard Prince laugh a few times. As the credits rolled, he rose without a word, skipping down the stairs and out of the theater, his sneakers shining laser-red in the darkness.

A LOT OF PRINCE ASSOCIATES HAVE A SIMILAR STORY:

They were never officially hired. Prince simply told you to show up again, and you did.

Two days after I returned from Minneapolis, Phaedra Ellis-Lamkins wrote to the agents at ICM: Prince was about to take Piano & A Microphone on tour in Australia. As long as it was okay with Random House, he wanted me to join him for the first leg, in Melbourne. With characteristic humbleness, he'd promised *The Sydney Morning Herald* that the shows would be "like watching me give birth to a new galaxy every night." The tour kicked off the following week. I packed my bags and told my boss I needed a week off to witness the birth of at least two new galaxies.

I arrived in Melbourne on February 16, the day of Prince's first show at the State Theatre. Kirk, who was staying in the room next door to mine at Crown Towers, told me I could expect a call from Prince under the alias Peter Bravestrong—his preferred pseudonym, apparently, for traveling incognito. Later, at Paisley, I'd see that even his luggage was tagged "Peter Bravestrong." I liked how obviously, almost defiantly, fictitious it sounded. Its comic-book gaudiness was in keeping with some of his past alter egos: Jamie Starr, Alexander Nevermind, Joey Coco. You could imagine them fighting crime together in a grim, neon city.

My room afforded a regal view of the Yarra River, trellised with bridges and decked out in red paper lanterns for the Lunar New Year. Around 12:30, the phone on my bedside table lit up with MR PETER BRAVESTRONG.

"Hi, Dan, it's Prince."

"Hello! How are you?"

"I've been better. I just got some sad news." I could tell. I asked what the matter was.

"It's, I'd—I'd rather not deal with it right now," he said. "I'm just going to get ready to play the show tonight, and I'll see you tomorrow?"

"Of course. That sounds fine."

He brightened a bit. "I have a lot of stuff to show you."

"I'm looking forward to it," I said.

"Okay, I'll see you at the show tonight. Goodbye."

I googled "Prince" and found news outlets reporting that Denise Matthews, better known as Vanity, was dead at fifty-seven—Prince's age. In the early eighties, the two had fallen in love, and Prince had tapped her to front the group Vanity 6. She was slated to appear in *Purple Rain* when their relationship fell apart.

Vanity's death shook Prince, and her memory loomed large at the first of the Piano & A Microphone shows at the State Theatre that evening. The stage set already had a touch of séance to it, though Prince might not endorse such an occultist comparison. Long, low tiers of candles burned at intervals around the piano, light poured in a velvety haze from the ceiling, and fractals purled and oozed on a screen at the back of the stage. As soon as he sat down at the piano and the cheers faded, he said: "I just found out someone dear to us has passed away. I'm gonna dedicate this song to her." He played a hybrid of "Little Red Corvette" and "Dirty Mind."

Later, during "The Ladder"—a song he'd written with his father—he made an on-the-fly adjustment to the lyrics: "He had a subject named Vanity. He loved her with a passion uncontested. But one day her smile went away."

The concert was nourishing. There was something wintry about it, or insular, that reminded me of people huddling for warmth against the cold. It was powerful to see Prince so visibly alone, figuring out what made his songs tick in real time. Whatever had compelled him to delete the bass line to "When Doves Cry" all those years ago was the same force moving him during these performances, showing off his flair for deconstruction, letting the crowd see the constituent pieces of his music. Sometimes he would leap up from the piano and walk away from it, like he was too much in awe of it. There was some stagecraft here, no doubt, but truth, too.

"I'm new to this playing alone," he said toward the end of the show. "I thank you all for being patient. I'm trying to stay focused—it's a little heavy for me tonight." He paused before beginning the next song: "The Beautiful Ones." "She knows about this one," he said.

THE NEXT DAY,

fortified with a carafe of coffee and the kind of room-service breakfast that delivers a day's supply of calories in one fell swoop, I followed Kirk up to Peter Bravestrong's suite, where Prince had secreted himself away in the bedroom. Kirk conferred in private with him—I actually never saw him face-to-face that afternoon. Instead, Kirk pointed me toward a desk in the main room, where I sat before an Office Depot legal pad with about thirty pages penciled in a messy script, rife with erasures and rewrites.

"He said he wants you to read that," Kirk said. "And then later he'll talk to you about it." There was a pad of hotel stationery nearby where I could leave questions for him. Kirk left me to it—he'd check in after half an hour or so.

The few people who've seen these pages since then have usually asked one question: How could I read them? Prince's handwriting was beautiful, with a fluidity that suggested it poured out of him almost involuntarily, like his music. But it also verged on illegible.

As it turned out, when you know that Prince is sitting in another room mere feet away—I could hear the TV, and occasional footsteps—waiting for your feedback, and that he's flown you halfway around the world just to garner that feedback, you can learn to read his handwriting very quickly. I found that it was almost like a Magic Eye illusion. Once you stared at it, the words coalesced in front of you.

And they were good words: the first chapters of his memoir.

Even in longhand, he wrote with his signature abbreviations, those precursors to textspeak he'd perfected back in the eighties: 👁 for I, U for you, R for are, and so on. I feared a distant showdown between author and publisher on this count—I could practically hear the tense phone call in which some industry bigwig tried to convince Prince that only the true devotees would suffer through hundreds of pages of 2s and Cs. Which side was 👁 on? Weirdly, after the first page, I was kind of into it. Though it seemed distant and alien at first, soon it helped me hear him.

I hadn't expected him to write anything at all, let alone something this assured. The pages were warm, funny, well observed, eloquent. I was floored. Given how scattered his conversation could sometimes become, his voice in these pages was surprisingly focused. This was Prince the raconteur, in a storytelling mode reminiscent of his more narrative songs, like "The Ballad of Dorothy Parker" or "Raspberry Beret," or the unreleased "Coco Boys."

He'd written about his childhood and adolescence in Minneapolis, starting with his first memory: his mother winking at him. I flipped through the pages to find a bevy of stories about his early life, all of them sensory, almost tactile. He recalled his favorite shirts of his dad's, the way his parents seemed to outdo each other sartorially. He summoned his first kiss, playing house with a girl in his neighborhood. He described the epilepsy he suffered as a kid. I'd worried that he'd shy away from more explicit details—he'd stopped playing his raciest hits—but his sexual development seemed very much on his mind. His first time feeling a girl up; his first time at an R-rated movie; a girlfriend slamming his locker shut, "like in a John Hughes film," just to hold mistletoe over his head and kiss him; it was all there, interspersed with his philosophy about music. "A good ballad should always put U in the mood 4 making love," he wrote.

I left a few questions and some compliments on the pad beside me, trying to keep it light—a litany of nitpicking seemed a sure way to get myself sent back to America prematurely. After I finished reading, Kirk took me to my room and told me to call Peter Bravestrong.

"So what'd you think?" Prince asked when he picked up.

"They're good. They're honestly really good. I'm not just saying this to inflate your ego."

"I don't think you could if you tried," he said with a laugh.

We touched on a few spots where I was confused or thought he could give the reader a better sense of place. He said he'd want me to draw him out on the bigger-picture stuff, too, and the exact timeline for the events he described.

"Coming at this as a songwriter, certain details don't feel relevant," he explained. He also worried that some passages might not sit well with certain readers, especially one on his aunt's excessive religion. "It could be—what's the word—polarizing. Maybe it's good to be polarizing, I don't know."

I told him it was definitely good—he'd written a song called "Controversy," after all. I wondered when he'd written so much, and how long it took. He'd only decided on an editor, a cowriter, and a concept in the past month. He hadn't even signed a contract yet. But his work, already so polished, seemed to have emerged overnight. A friend would later tell me Prince was so excited about these pages that he'd read passages to her over the phone.

"Why don't you call Random House," he said. "Tell them we need some money for this thing, so we can announce it and start preselling it—because that will move tickets. I can feel myself getting amped up about this." And so could I: Whatever listlessness he'd felt yesterday had dissipated.

"Anyway, thanks for coming all the way out here," he said.

"Oh, no problem," I said automatically. I did not ask him why I'd spent roughly twenty-three hours in the air just to conduct a meeting with him over the phone.

Fortunately, there was more to come. That night I returned to the State Theatre for the later Piano & A Microphone show. True to form, he'd switched up the set list, and he'd worked in some new stories throughout. He recalled the enchanting sight of his father's right hand playing the piano—his desperation to be able to do that—and the interior life he'd developed at a young age, set against the rhythm of North Minneapolis. On interminable Sunday mornings, he'd have to sit through church and a trip to the bakery afterward. "What you hear is true. Black church services last too long." "Are we there yet?" he remembered asking. Meaning: home, where he could watch *The Wizard of Oz* and try to figure out why he liked "Over the Rainbow" so much.

"I was studying my father, studying my mother," he said. "If you know where you're from, know what time it is, you'll get where you're going."

After the show, Kirk texted. Prince wanted me at the after-party, which would soon be underway at Aria, a waterfront bar. I showed up to find a well-heeled crowd already swarming the place, which was swathed in purple light for the occasion. A line stretched around the corner. Inside, it was chintzed out with faux-crystal chandeliers and, over the bartenders, the same stock photo of a Red Bull and vodka, repeated three times. The room had the tense, promissory energy of a New Year's Eve party at 11:30, with the caveat that midnight—in this case, Prince—might never come.

Maybe ninety minutes later, Prince strutted in through the back entrance—his cane enhanced his royal affect—and beckoned to me from the other side of a velvet rope.

"I was in a different mood tonight," Prince said when I asked him how he felt about the show. He'd been happier, less aware of himself. We were seated on a plush couch with a marble tray of chocolate-covered strawberries in front of us, and Kirk standing guard; the concert's promoters sat on the other side. Prince managed the not-uncomplicated task of carrying on conversations with all of us at once, all while bobbing his head more than negligibly to the Ohio Players and giving the crowd something to cheer about.

"I was happy to hear 'Purple Music,'" I said. It was an unreleased track from 1982 in perennial circulation among bootleggers—and, by coincidence, the one I'd listened to most since I'd first found out that I was up for the cowriting job.

Prince nodded. He seemed happy I'd recognized it. "That was the first time I've played that song live," he said. "Someone said they recorded it. I might just release it."

But that expansive attitude didn't apply to every song in his backlist. When the DJ put on "Head," one of his more obscene numbers, he had it turned off right away. Then he wanted to talk business. He sat forward and gripped his cane with both hands. He was wearing black leather gloves with his symbol on them.

"Have you talked to Random House?"

I said I'd told them about the pages he wrote.

"You have power now," he said. "Learn to wield it. It's you, it's me, and it's them. Convince them that they need to put everything behind me. Even just for a little. I don't want them publishing this like it's some book of poetry."

"They won't," I said. "Even if you think that book publishing can be sleepy—"

"Not anymore," he said. He locked eyes with me. "I trust you. Tell them I trust you."

I was awed and overwhelmed. It felt like I'd wandered onto the path of someone else's life, and that, sooner or later, some cosmic course correction would ensure that things went back to normal. I ate a chocolate-covered strawberry.

"I'll look at your notes and address them point by point. Get a stenographer," he told me. "I'd prefer it to be a woman. Or—you can just type it yourself. I'll give you the pages. I'll trust you with the paper."

He went out and danced with the crowd for a minute, then popped back behind the velvet rope. After whispering and smiling with Kirk, he pointed his head toward a woman wearing a leopard-print dress: "Kirk says he wants you to get Leopard Print's phone number." He brought her up again a few minutes later. "Shouldn't you be out there dancing with Leopard Print? Are you married?"

What a strange thing trust is, I thought. Prince had promised to give me the first and only pages he'd written about his life; he didn't even know if I was married. I found this heartening. Maybe it was cavalier, but all he needed in the way of a background check was a long, honest conversation with someone.

At about three in the morning, we left Aria through the kitchen. In the service garage, an Audi SUV was waiting for us. Prince and I sat in the back as we drove through the hush of Melbourne in the wee hours. After the unrelenting volume and histrionics of the bar, the silence was welcome; I found I had nothing to say that was worth breaking it. Prince gazed out the window at the shuttered shops, the empty streets. I felt like we were the only people in the city.

"We should do a golden ticket promotion," he said after a few minutes of quiet. "Put the book together with some other prize—maybe we play a concert for the winner. Make the winner tell their own story."

He sounded exhausted, like he couldn't turn his mind off. It was always working through things like this: The promotion of the project, the project's reception in the world, existed parallel to the thing itself for him. He would discuss the marketing of the book as often as the writing, always with a nimble, try-anything-once approach to entrepreneurship that reminded me of an effective small business owner more than an international superstar.

The car pulled in to Crown Towers through a VIP entrance that snaked below the hotel to a secret bank of underground elevators. Of course such places existed; of course I'd never thought to consider that they did. A doorman stationed at the elevator welcomed us back.

"I won't let you get lost," Kirk said as we soared upward. The silence felt even more total now.

"I like the quiet of hotels at this hour," I said. "All the long carpeted corridors, no one around. There's something weirdly appealing about wandering hotel halls late at night."

Prince gave a sly smile. "I've done it many times."

ON FRIDAY,

we arranged for Prince to give me what Kirk called "the tools that you need." He led me back to Peter Bravestrong's suite—or "villa," as Crown Towers branding referred to it—and what I thought would be a simple handoff became a two-hour conversation, the most probing, unguarded talk we ever had. Prince, wearing a loose-fitting rainbow-colored top with his face and afro on it, sat me down at the same desk where I'd read his pages. There were a few packs of hairnets off to the side. "Sit here," he said again, bringing over a pen and paper. He encouraged me to take notes; sometimes he even told me to be sure I'd written something down.

He wondered how I thought the book should begin: if it'd be best to start in the middle with a story or at the beginning. We could even have a story on the cover, if we wanted. And should it start with his voice or mine? I said I thought it was simplest to start at the beginning—that he'd chosen a lovely opening, with his mother's eyes.

"Music is healing," he said. "Write that down first." This was to be our guiding principle. "Music holds things together."

Then we went through what he'd written page by page, addressing the notes I'd left and talking about his story more broadly.

As we spoke, Prince, in higher spirits than I'd ever seen him before, began to improvise about all the shapes the book could take, all it could contain, the message it could deliver. Since we'd spoken at Paisley, his ambitions had been amplified tenfold—an impressive feat, given that he'd started off wanting to end racism. "The book should be a handbook for the brilliant community: wrapped in autobiography, wrapped in biography," he said. "It should teach that what you create is yours. Say, 'We've got this if we're left alone.'" He remembered "a dude in my community ten times smarter than me," though he didn't want to name him in the book. "What if *he* had the opportunities the Bush daughters had?" It was incumbent on us to help people, especially young black artists, realize the power and agency they had.

I liked the idea of regarding the memoir as a kind of hand-book. It was a perfect way to expand its remit, to add another dimension to its storytelling. And it gave another layer of meaning to the title, *The Beautiful Ones,* which could now denote an entire community of creators—the song did contain the lines "Paint a perfect picture / bring to life a vision in one's mind . . ." (I know what you're thinking. Just don't pay attention to the lyrics that come next.)

"Keep what you make," Prince said more than once. "I stayed in Minneapolis because Minneapolis made me. You have to give back. My dad came to Minneapolis from Cotton Valley, Louisiana. He learned in the harshest conditions what it means to control wealth. 'Black Muse' is about that, creating wealth in the inner city," he said, referring to a song on his new album, *HITnRUN Phase Two.* "Stopping eminent domain."

He wanted to teach readers about Black Wall Street, a well-spring of black entrepreneurship that flourished in Tulsa, Oklahoma in the early twentieth century. After the Civil War, as freed blacks flocked to booming Tulsa and bought land, segregation forced them to the city's Greenwood neighborhood, where their proprietorship and ingenuity created a thriving community. Soon Greenwood boasted hundreds of black-owned businesses, plus nearly two dozen churches, a school, and a public library. It became one of the first and most essential examples of black prosperity in the United States. "It's amazing," Prince said, "the wealth amassing. I love reading about the Civil War and the amassing of wealth, when the South became wealthier than Britain." Then came Tulsa's 1921 race massacre: Their hatred fanned by accusations that a black boy had raped a white girl, thousands of armed whites doused Greenwood in kerosene and burned it down block by block, looting and plundering as they went. Hundreds died; thousands more lost their homes. Black Wall Street was decimated.

"The Fountainhead," Prince said. "Did you read that? What'd you think of it?" I said I didn't like it—that I had no patience for objectivism, nor for Ayn Rand's present-day acolytes, with their almost farcical devotion to the free market and unfettered individualism. Prince agreed, though he saw how the philosophy could be seductive. "I watched the movie, old, black-and-white, where he gives the speech at the end about burning down the building and the blueprints. . . ." It was a pivotal moment in Randian philosophy: "No work is ever done collectively," her character Howard Roark sneers. Prince worried that too much of hip-hop was in the thrall of ideas like Rand's, dedicated more to cutthroat self-absorption than a spirit of community.

"We need a book that talks to the aristocrats," he said. "Not just the fans. We have to dismantle *The Fountainhead* brick by brick. It's like the aristocrat's bible. It's a compound of problems. They basically want to eliminate paradise. What about white supremacy, and what it has in common with objectivism? Is it satanic? Is it really the greater good? We should attack the whole notion of supremacy." The purity of its original meaning had been corrupted, he thought. "There used to be *bands* called the Supremes! Supremacy is about, everything flourishes, everything is nourished."

That's why he felt he needed my voice in the book, too: A radical call for collective ownership, for black creativity, couldn't be made alone. "When I say, 'I own *Purple Rain*,' I sound . . . like Kanye." He paused. "Who I consider a friend." The problem was that statements of ownership too often read as self-aggrandizing. It was more powerful to hear them from other people. "*You* need to say I own *Purple Rain*," he said—though he was still amazed that there could be any dissenting opinion on the subject. "For someone to say, 'I control *Purple Rain*,' it's—blasphemous."

To that end, he wanted to find some formal devices that would make the book unique, a symbiosis of his words and mine, its authorship in a state of flux. "It would be dope if, toward the end, our voices started to blend," he said. "In the beginning they're distinct, but by the end we're both writing." When we discussed the passage he'd written about his childhood bouts with epilepsy, he said, "I'm just vamping here. We could use seizures as a way of blending our voices. Blackouts. 'Here comes another blackout.'"

I was exhilarated. We were on our way to building something unique, a memoir that defied conventions. He was already thinking about what the cover might be. He'd had a new passport photo taken, and it had gone viral. Of course it had: His lips in a gentle pout, his eyeliner perfect, every hair in his moustache manicured to perfection, he seemed to be daring the customs officials of the world to give him a kiss instead of a stamp. "I asked Meron—you know Meron, right?—to make sure it was on my actual passport. She said, 'I did it.' Then I tweeted it and they featured it on CNN and in *Time* magazine. Maybe we should have that on the cover," he joked, "with all my info and stuff. We need this to get weird."

There was a strong positive energy in the room. A lot of laughter. A sense that we were going to surprise people. "Brother to brother," Prince said, "it's good to be controversial." This was a confident about-face from his remarks a few days ago. "We were brought together to do this. There was a process of elimination. To do this, it takes a personality not fighting against what I'm trying to do. You know a lot more words than I do. Write this thing like you want to win the Pulitzer and then—" He pantomimed smashing the Pulitzer on the desk.

Comparing me to Norman Mailer trying to understand Muhammad Ali, he said, "I can tell you're like one of those sixties rock writers. You need to go into your third eye. . . . It's good to see that you're willing to take the plunge. Because people are gonna ask questions."

He thumbed about half of the pages he'd written, tore them out of the legal pad, and gave them to me, urging me to write more on—anything. "I'll keep going with my stuff but you, you've got the good stuff. I'm excited about that." He stood and we walked to the door of the Bravestrong Villa.

"This was helpful to me," he said. "I have a clearer understanding of what we have to do. Talk to Chris and Random House. Tell me what they say."

He gave me a hug goodbye. "Talk to you soon."

Suddenly my nose was in his hair, and I could smell his perfume. You could never *not* smell his perfume, granted, but now it was on me—I spent the rest of the day catching whiffs of him, trying to process all of it, everything he'd said. I don't know how to describe the scent: I can't say that it had top notes of cinnamon or anything like that. It was just *his,* his scent, in that proprietary-olfactory way. I was in the antipodes and I smelled like Prince. What? How? It put me in mind of the first line from "Mountains": "Once upon a time, in a land called fantasy . . ."

I'd always known that Prince had a lot of protégés; I'd never thought about why, really. He was a preternatural talent, and, more cynically, it was an easy way for him to charm women. But plenty of brilliant musicians never took anyone under their wings. It'd never occurred to me that grooming artists took some didactic skill, some specific subvariety of leadership. Prince understood the delicate mechanism of self-confidence. He could quell the chorus of doubts in people's heads—could make you settle into your own potential. Later I'd read something that Gwen Stefani remembered him saying: "'Have you ever just tried writing a hit? Like, don't just try writing a song, try and write a hit song.' I remember him saying that and me thinking, Yeah, you're right. Why would you write anything else?"

"If I want this book to be about one overarching thing," Prince told me that day, "it's freedom. And the freedom to create autonomously. Without anyone telling you what to do or how or why." It was summer in Melbourne, and the next day I'd be back on a plane to frigid New York. I spent hours walking along the sunny river with his words in my head, listening to the Ohio Players' "Skin Tight" at a deafening volume. ("The bass & drums on this record would make Stephen Hawking dance," Prince had written in the pages he showed me. "No disrespect— it's just that funky.") I guess I looked like I knew where I was going; tourists kept stopping me to ask for directions.

ONCE
I GOT
BACK TO
NEW
YORK,

I didn't see Prince for a little more than a month. Through Kirk, he'd email me things: fawning reviews of his shows, an insightful NPR piece about his vexed relationship with technology, an Instagram photo of him, a tweet about him. Meanwhile, he was in the midst of tense negotiations with Random House. His book contract was deviating far from the boilerplate, and there was still no guarantee that he'd sign it at all. At one point, he called Chris Jackson, his editor, at home, and asked if they could just publish the book without contracts or lawyers. As Chris recalled: "I said I'd love to, but the company can't cut a check without a contract in place. He paused and said, 'I'll call you back.' And he did—with some fine points for the contract."

As the back-and-forth stretched into mid-March, Prince began to dangle the possibility of a surprise event in New York. If they could wrap up negotiations by Friday, March 18, they could announce the memoir at a secret concert that very night. With the day approaching, staffers at Random House and ICM made frantic arrangements for a location and cobbled together an invitation list. There was one contractual sticking point to resolve before the announcement: Prince wanted to reserve the right to pull the book from shelves, permanently, at any time in the future, should he ever feel that it no longer reflected who he was. The question was how much he'd have to pay Random

House to do so. On Friday, after a three-or-four-day volley of offers and counteroffers, they settled on a figure, and Prince hopped on a plane. At 4:40 P.M., he tweeted, "Y IS PRINCE IN NEW YORK RIGHT NOW?!"

By eight that evening, a crowd of maybe a hundred and fifty people had convened to hear the answer. He made the announcement at Avenue, a narrow, dusky club on Tenth Avenue, in Chelsea. His friend Harry Belafonte was in attendance, as were Spike Lee, Trevor Noah, Gayle King, Maxwell, and the cast of *Hamilton*. He'd also brought along his personal DJ, Pam the Funkstress—or Purple Pam, as he called her—who was spinning eighties-era tracks that made the walls shake. As usual, cellphones were forbidden, but complimentary glasses of champagne were on offer at the bar. Prince's publicist had told me that my name would probably be kept out of the announcement; I wasn't supposed to talk to the media, and I'd signed a nondisclosure agreement. Still, I was nervous. I'd never been in a situation where it was even possible that I'd be buttonholed by reporters.

The lights flashed red and the music stopped. Prince descended a stairway high above the crowd and stood at the second-floor balcony, leaning on its Plexiglas barrier. I saw Kirk and Meron with him. In effulgent gold and purple stripes, looming over us, he looked like a nobleman prepared to address the peasantry.

"You all still read books, right?" he asked. The crowd cheered. "The good people of Random House have made me an offer I can't refuse." He was writing a memoir. "This is my first. My brother Dan is helping me with it. He's a good critic, and that's what I need. He's not a yes-man at all, and he's really helping me get through this," Prince said.

"We're starting from the beginning, from my first memory, and hopefully we can go all the way up to the Super Bowl," he said. This was news to me—we'd never discussed the Super Bowl. "We're working as fast as we can. The working title is *The Beautiful Ones*." The spotlight on him was glaring; he took out a pair of bulbous sunglasses that looked like arachnid eyes. "Now I can see better," he said, putting them on. "I literally just got off the plane. I'm gonna go home and change and put some dancing clothes on. Props to my brother Harry Belafonte."

He disappeared and the music started again. I stood there in a daze, failing to recognize at least three people I'd met multiple times before. It was real now—he'd said it—and soon, I imagined, we'd go off somewhere and apply ourselves to the messy, heady task of getting his life on paper.

A short while later, Prince returned and began his performance. The forty-five-minute show was what Prince enthusiasts had come to call "the sampler set," in which he cued up the backing tracks to a medley of his greatest hits and sang live over them. Everybody danced; my mood buoyed. The songs were peppered with such Princely interjections as "We want to thank Random House. Ain't nothing random about this funk!" and "Check your mailbox. There might be some funk in there." I still hear him saying it when I check my mail. Not nearly often enough is any funk to be found.

THE NEXT DAY,

as news of the memoir caromed around the Internet, Kirk invited me to join him, Meron, and Prince at The Groove, a nightclub in the West Village. Li'nard's Many Moods, fronted by a prodigious bassist named Li'nard Jackson, was playing there. We met around midnight. Prince's security detail had reserved a high-backed banquette toward the back, facing the stage but just out of sight of the dance floor, thus ensuring that Prince—when he arrived holding a jacket over his head, sandwiched between Kirk and Meron—was hiding in plain sight. He had me scooch in beside him and cupped my ear again. I wondered what percentage of his conversations occurred over loud music.

"Did you get paid yet?" he asked.

"No," I said.

"Me either."

I was confused—the contract hadn't even been signed. But this was one of the cornerstones of his contractual philosophy, was it not? The artist should always be paid; the company should always be paying. By this point it was an almost calming refrain. In Prince's world, questions of money, usually so crass, had an air of scrappy anti-corporate camaraderie. Money meant that we were in this together. (At his final show a few weeks later, he'd play one of his favorite covers: the Staples Singers' "When Will We Be Paid?" He'd described it to a friend as the narrative of the book.)

38

He'd just seen *Hamilton,* and he was jazzed on it. "It's a diverse cast, even though they're telling a European story. You trust them to talk about race and stuff." It had given him a thought about the book. "It should be paced like a Broadway play, with lots of dialogue. Just—right into it. No need to linger on anything."

The band hadn't started yet, and Michael Jackson's "Bad" came on the speaker system. Prince said it reminded him of a story of the one time they were supposed to work together. "I'll have to tell you about that later. There are gonna be some bombshells in this thing. I hope people are ready. We need our own publicity team to hype this book—because it'll live up to the hype."

The next song was by Alexander O'Neal, which prompted a memory, too. "He was supposed to be the lead singer of the Time. But he had all these personal problems—he'd be onstage sweating before the first song started." He started to say more, but cut himself off. Purple Pam, his DJ, had joined us, and he had a few words of advice. First: It was always a good idea to close a set with "September," by Earth, Wind & Fire. Second: No profanity. "These DJs play songs with cussing and then they wonder why fights break out in the clubs. You set the soundtrack for it!"

I asked him about the Super Bowl—I was surprised he'd brought it up as an endpoint to the book. "I was thinking maybe we start it there, actually. Me on stage—what it feels like to get to that point. And then flash back to my mother."

The band came on. Li'nard caught Prince out of the corner of his eye and gave him a knowing, appreciative look. They brought a guest vocalist onstage; he was sensational. "That's what's wrong with the music industry right there," Prince told me. Why would a record label put their weight behind artists who can't sing when talent like this was out there? "That guy—we could record a hit single with him in five minutes."

We sat back and enjoyed the music. I'd never sat this close to Prince, and I tried to get some good sidelong glances at him when I could. He looked weary, but happy—happy, but weary. Every so often he'd whisper something to Meron that made her crack up. "She's got this laugh that, once you get her going, you wouldn't believe," he told me. With everyone's eyes on the stage, and a banquette that soared high above his afro, no one even noticed he was there.

About two thirds of the way through the set, he nodded to Kirk. It was time to go. "So what we'll do is—you free in about a week? We'll get together wherever we're playing and really start to work on this thing. I want to put the Piano & A Microphone tour on hold to really work on this." Their car was outside. He shook my hand, gave me a quick side hug, and hustled out holding his jacket over his head. The crowd at the bar didn't give him a second glance.

BUT A WEEK WENT BY,

and then another, with no word. In early April, Kirk asked me if I could resend the typed pages with my notes. I did, but nothing more came of it. The silence began to concern me, especially as I read that Prince had postponed a show in Atlanta. I didn't know it yet, but I'd seen him for the last time.

At least he'd signed the contract for the book—kind of. Forever leery of the dotted line, he'd authorized his lawyer, Phaedra Ellis-Lamkins, with a one-time power of attorney, granting her the right to sign the publishing agreement in his stead. A notary arrived at Paisley Park and collected his signature on April 7, the same day he'd canceled the Atlanta show, claiming illness. ("DESPITE INFLUENZA, THIS PLANET IS PRICELESS!" he'd tweeted a few days earlier.)

Which brings me back to our final conversation, four days before he died. We were on the subject of his parents again, dissecting their dueling influence in his life. He felt it on a biological level—hence his interest in cellular memory. Was it possible that his body bore the scars of theirs?

"Thinking about the structure of the book," he said, "it would be dope if, in your voice, you got scientific, fact-based—asking questions but also laying down the facts about cellular memory. While I write about my life, music, and the street life. And thinking about 'When Doves Cry'—we could break that song down lyric by lyric." There was some way, too, that funk music was the ideal vehicle for this dilemma of his. He was a living contradiction, his mother and his father in one. Funk worked the same way, fusing impulse to structure. That's why we had to find a word for it.

He'd been mulling over the cover, too. "I had this artist draw me in phases through my career. Hang on, I'll send it to you." These were the famous designs from Martin Homent, who'd illustrated "The Many Faces of Prince" throughout his career. Maybe it would make a good cover. It was all something to consider for "when we really start working on it." But this time, there was no date attached to that work.

"Really, I just wanted to call and let you know that that's what I've been thinking about," he said. "And I'm okay."

We hung up. It felt to me like our most normal, natural conversation yet, even if, as I wrote earlier, I spent the majority of it in an ungainly crouch on my bedroom floor. We'd picked up right where we left off.

Late in the morning of April 21, I was on a Metro-North train to Connecticut with a friend when the text messages began to come in. TMZ was reporting a fatality at Paisley Park. The Carver County Sheriff's Office was on the scene. I didn't think it could be Prince. Looking back, I'm embarrassed by how credulous I was, by how fuzzy my reasoning had become. But Prince had told me that he was okay, and I took him at his word.

I kept refreshing the news sites. Soon the headlines increased their point size, and the trickle of text messages became a deluge. Prince was dead. Outside, spring had come, and through the train window I watched the landscape scroll by at a stately pace, the first buds of the season beginning to bloom, acres of brown earth now mottled with green. The Metro-North car was thick with commuters, all of them going about their business as normal. As my friend and I began to talk in increasingly panicked tones, a few of them shot us shushing looks. I wanted to grab these people by the lapels and shake them. Did they not know that one of the greatest artists of our time was dead? Did they not understand the gravity of this situation? My mind felt like something you'd smear on a cracker, and I didn't want to start crying, not here, because once I started, I wouldn't stop. Journalists began to call *The Paris Review* offices, seeking comment and inviting me on the air. Old teachers, friends of friends, ex-bandmates—anyone with the slightest connection to him was trotted out to register the same shock and despair. The wall-to-wall news coverage only had the effect of making it seem less real. And no one could say what had happened.

Getting the job with him had sent my daydreams into overdrive. Because if this was possible, what wasn't? I could imagine something absurd, like opening a bookshop with Prince or touring Europe with him, and now it was much more plausible. My baseline was all out of whack. I'd just accepted that our book was real. Now reality was putting my imagination in check, and my entire three months with him had the contours of a dream. I was grieving as a fan, a collaborator, and a friend. The coming days brought distressing rumors of addiction, first in the harsh block-capital exclamations of tabloids and later in more sober reporting. This was the first of many blows. Soon it would come out that he'd died of an accidental fentanyl overdose, having taken counterfeit Vicodin pills laced with the much stronger opioid. Though fentanyl has since sadly become a household name, it wasn't part of the national conversation when it was linked to Prince.

As I read more about his last months, it was hard to reconcile the sunny, puckish, solicitous man I met with one who could be unyielding or willfully opaque. One of the people closest to him told detectives that, after his last show in Atlanta, he'd said that he "enjoyed sleeping more these days," and that maybe it meant he'd done all he was supposed to do on Earth; waking life was "incredibly boring." I found those words wrenching when I read them, a disavowal of everything we'd talked about. Then I remembered that he'd said essentially the same thing at the first Piano & A Microphone show: "I like dreaming now more than I used to. Some of my friends have passed away, and I see them in my dreams. It's like they are here, and the dreams are just like waking sometimes." What I'd found unendurable in one context was beautiful to me in another.

There was nothing false in the way he spoke to me, and nothing false in the way he spoke during his darkest moments. I can't think less of him for feeling enervated, depleted, for hiding his pain, for telling me he was okay when he wasn't. He was living on his own terms. To expect anything more of him would be to expect magic: rightfully, his least favorite word.

BECAUSE PRINCE DIED

without a will, a Carver County District Court judge appointed a special administrator, Bremer Trust, to run his estate. Prince had kept a bank account with Bremer for many years; they were headquartered in St. Paul. And one of their first priorities, given the sizable tax bill the estate was facing, was to monetize Prince's assets however they could. As it happened, the book had been one of the last projects he'd finalized with a contract. With that in mind, representatives from Bremer got in touch with Random House: Was there any way the book was still possible? Their preliminary walk-through of Paisley had revealed a wealth of unseen photos, papers, and ephemera. Did we want to fly out and have a look at it?

We did. In late June, I made the trip to Chanhassen along with Chris Jackson, Dan Kirschen, and Julie Grau, the publisher of Spiegel & Grau. Though local police and DEA agents had removed a few items relevant to their investigations, Paisley was otherwise exactly as Prince had left it, and his aura was everywhere. Back in Melbourne, he'd given me the first ten pages of his memoir—I hoped the rest was at Paisley, and that maybe he'd written more.

Employees from Bremer led us through the compound, though they were still getting their bearings themselves. Quintessentially Midwestern and unfailingly polite, they spoke of Prince with reverence and, occasionally, bewilderment, as they attempted to divine the meaning behind some of the choices he'd made. The security cameras had all been disabled and were sometimes pointing inward, toward the wall. Smoke alarms had been taped up. The fabled vault had suffered water damage. Some of the Bremer visitors sounded like archaeologists excavating an ancient site they'd discovered. "We think this is where he . . ."

Still, the overall mood was one of somber respect. Bremer had maintained Prince's onsite dietary restrictions, so we brought in vegan lunches from a local co-op. We were left almost unattended as we roamed from room to room. There were wonders at every turn. Prince had preserved much of his creative process in amber, or its purple equivalent. Notes and lyrics were scrawled on envelopes, on the backs of receipts, on hotel stationery from far-flung nations. Proofs and contact sheets from his photo shoots were ubiquitous, his favorite selections marked with grease pencil. Enormous wheeled suitcases, some of them tagged "Peter Bravestrong," were unzipped to reveal makeup compacts and a superabundance of cosmetics. Pearlescent guitar picks emblazoned with his symbol were always within arm's reach. In the garage, a stash of CDs was spread across the floor—I noticed *A Decade of Steely Dan* on top—and boxes of his 1996 wedding program remained untouched. A set of his-and-hers bowling balls (engraved for ♀ and his wife, Mayte, respectively) were still in their leather carrying case. Once, in the upstairs room he used as his office, I walked by one of the shirts he'd worn, smelled his perfume, and had to sit down. It was like he was there again.

The anteroom to the vault functioned as an archive in and of itself, with framed photos and stacked recordings. And Bremer had found boxes of material pertaining to the *Purple Rain* film: forms with the exact lines recorded for ADR (automated dialogue replacement), continuity Polaroids from the set, pictures from location scouts, various drafts of the script.

In a big white bedroom that had the cryptic phrase *Everything U Think Is True* painted on the wall, he'd put aside a cache of handwritten lyrics to his best-known songs, clipped together and seemingly waiting to be found. As we lay on the white carpet marveling at the cross-outs and rewrites in Prince's lyrics, one of Bremer's representatives approached and brandished a notepad. She'd found the rest of the memoir pages I'd read in Australia. I sighed with relief. Though Prince hadn't added anything new to the notepad, I'd been worried that it would never turn up.

And then the vault: The vast majority of it was given over to reels of tape. But in a few steel cabinets toward the front, he'd set aside a few things that jumped out at us right away. Photos and mementos from his childhood, many of them from the same years he'd written about in his memoir pages. Everything was gingerly preserved: early press clippings, his father's wallet, even a report card from junior high. We were stunned. "I don't live in the past," Prince had told *Rolling Stone* back in 1985. And yet he'd held on to so much, as if in anticipation of the retrospective turn he'd take with Piano & A Microphone and *The Beautiful Ones*.

We didn't want to publish a book simply because we could. And we had no desire to print anything that wandered from the guidelines Prince had discussed with Chris and me. The vastness of his archive gave us hope. There was a way to realize his ambitions without compromising the integrity of the project, and without making something that felt merely like a slapped-together piece of tour merchandise. If we included only objects that he'd held on to, we'd know that we had something authentic on our hands. Everything that spoke to us was something that Prince had kept. The book could be in his voice, under his authorship, with as few incursions as possible from outside sources. Under no condition did we want to put words in his mouth, or to sow any confusion about what he'd said and written.

But we needed more time. The four of us returned to Paisley in July, going through it again room by room, more deliberately this time. The air-conditioning had broken down, and the place was stiflingly hot. We logged long hours, flagging items that could be marshaled into some narrative about Prince's life, bringing them together in the same conference room where he'd hosted the editors, and where he and I had first spoken.

As the estate's plans shifted to other creative projects, including opening a Paisley Park museum and throwing a memorial concert, inertia set in. I'd returned the sheaf of memoir pages he'd entrusted to me—about a third of the total—to the estate, and I began to worry that they'd never see the light of day. I remember dropping them off at FedEx, wondering if I was making a huge mistake. They were my most cherished possession.

But in 2017, when Comerica Bank took over as the estate's administrator, we found momentum again. With the assistance of the estate's new archivists, we reviewed more than 5,200 items from Prince's collection. We were on the lookout for objects that gave us the same frisson we'd felt when we met him: things that communicated some intimacy; that shed a new light on his family and his art; that demonstrated his creative process, and, as he desired, would make his readers want to create, too.

In the meantime, the estate had released Prince's first official posthumous single, a song called "Moonbeam Levels," recorded in 1982. "Yesterday I tried 2 write a novel," it starts, "but I didn't know where to begin." I could relate. There was so much to say, but finding a viable structure for it was next to impossible. Even when Prince was alive, we'd promised a book that would deliver "an unconventional and poetic journey through his life and creative work." Now the question was how far we could wander from convention before the journey went off the rails.

I kept going back to lines from "Moonbeam Levels," in which Prince sings of a man who never kept a diary—who only wished to "fight 4 perfect love." It was true. Of the thousands of papers we reviewed, not one of them resembled a diary. There was, however, plenty of evidence of Prince fighting for perfect love. It was never too late.

PRINCE HAD WANTED A STORY

that went "all the way to the Super Bowl," but in his absence, there was no way to produce such a book without deviating from the course he'd set out, making too many assumptions, leaving too many omissions. The memoir pages we worked on covered his childhood and adolescence, leading into the foothills of his career. His paper trail picked up there, cutting an oblique path toward the pinnacle of *Purple Rain*. That path was the heart of the book, we thought. Call it an origin tale: the story of how Prince became Prince.

We settled on a book anchored by four points, all linked by the handwritten lyrics that testified to his creative process. First, this introduction, telling the story of how any of this came to pass in the first place. Second, the pages Prince had written expressly for his memoir, a love letter to his parents supplemented with the expansions and asides he'd made to me when we went through his words together in Melbourne.

Third, one of the most affecting items in the archive: a photo book Prince had started to keep in December 1977, when he was nineteen and staying in San Francisco to record his debut album, *For You*. The photos he kept chronicled his first record deal with Warner Bros., his trips to California, and the caring community he was part of in Minneapolis—the people who made it possible for him to create. Some of them were still on his mind many decades later: He'd written about them in his memoir pages. Captioned in his own hand, the photo album brimmed with his youthful swagger and his sense of humor; it captured the unbridled potential of someone who had a free hand to make art the way he wanted to make it. If one of Prince's goals for *The Beautiful Ones* was to demonstrate that an artist is in a constant state of becoming, always imagining himself into the future, then this photo album was a crystalline example of his self-conception at the outset of his career. Fittingly, it ended in April 1978—the month his first album came out.

Fourth and finally, we found a handwritten synopsis he'd made for the film that would become *Purple Rain*. Written sometime between the spring of 1982 and early 1983—before the movie had a director, a screenwriter, or even a name, and before he'd written the song "Purple Rain"—these pages find him working through the major themes and characters of the movie. They're a testament to his creative energy. At the time, he'd just had his first top-ten hit with "Little Red Corvette," and he was determined to make a big movie, something with high stakes and drama in addition to music and comedy. This story continues the discussion we'd started about his parents, who are more than ever at the center of his psychology here. Prince owned *Purple Rain:* It was in and of his DNA. Reading his first ideas about the film, you can see how his genius sprung from the conflict of his mother and father—"one of my life's dilemmas," as he told me—becoming a creative source that he would revisit throughout his life.

Anyone who knew Prince knew that it was never a good idea to guess how he'd feel about something. But insofar as he envisioned this book as a collaborative project, I believe this is the closest, truest realization of the work that we started during those three whirlwind months in 2016. It asks the reader to fill in the gaps, to imagine a way into the negative space. If it raises as many questions as it answers, so much the better—his intention was never to puncture the veil of mystery around him.

For the rest of my life, I'll wonder what sort of book Prince and I would've written had he remained alive. These pages represent only a sliver of what could've been—and this book is, in its very existence, an expression of grief as much as a celebration of life. But I hope it makes good on the mission he set out for us: to provide "a handbook for the brilliant community, wrapped in autobiography, wrapped in biography," a book that blended our voices to tell a story, his story, with purpose.

By now you must know what that purpose is. I hope you're ready to give yourself over to it. "Try to create," Prince told me that day in Melbourne. "I want to tell people to create. Just start by creating your day. Then create your life."

—Dan Piepenbring

PART I.

THE
BEAUTIFUL
ONES

1.

My Mother's Eyes

That's the 1st thing Eye can Remember.
U know how U can tell when someone
is smiling just by looking in their eyes?
That was my Mother's Eyes.
Sometime She would squint them
like She was about 2 tell U a Secret.
& I found out later my Mother had a lot
of secrets.

My Father's Piano. That's the 1st thing Eye
Remember hearing. As a younger Man
His playing was very busy but Precise. It
was a joyous sound.

The Eyes & the Ears of a Songwriter
can never get enough praise. The way things
look & the way things sound, when conveyed
lyrically can give a song space & gravity.

Of course 2 the writer there was
nothing more beautiful than His Mother's Eyes
but Y? One of the reasons is how playful
they were. The fun & mischief they promised.

There were 2 princes in the House where
We lived. The older one with all the
responsibilities of heading a household & the
younger one who's only mode of operandis
was Fun. Not just any run-of-the-mill
childhood board game fun, but fun with a

wink attached. My mother liked 2 wink at Me. Eye knew what a wink meant b4 Eye knew how 2 spell My name. A wink meant something covert was going on. Something special that only those who were in on it could attest. Sometimes when My Father wasn't paying attention He'd say something 2 My Mother, & She would wink at me.

She never told me what it meant & sometimes it would b accompanied by a gentle caress of her hand 2 my face but Eye am quite sure now this is the birth of My physical Imagination.

An entire world of secrets & intrigue 2 solve & good old fashioned make-believe. A place where everything 4 a change goes ur way. One could get used 2 this. Many artists fell down the rabbit holes of their own imaginations & never return. There have been many who decry this as self-destruction but Eye prefer the term FREE-WILL. Life is better lived. What path one takes is what sets us apart from the rest.

Those who be different 'r the ones most interesting 2 us.

A vibrant imagination is where the best songs & sound. Make-believe characters wearing make-believe clothes all 2gether creating memories & calling it Life.

My parents were beautiful. 2 watch them leave the crib — dressed up 4 a night on the town was one of my favorite things 2 do. Even tho my mother was walking funny when she came home it was all worth 2 me just 2 c them happy.

Whenever they were happy w/ the one another all was right the world.

Thinking back, my father's mood used 2 change instantly whenever my Mother was dressed up.

She craved attention & he gave her plenty of it when she was sharp. Of all the family friends & relatives my parents were the sharpest! No one could accessorize like they could. My Mother's jewelry, gloves & hats all had 2 match. My father's cuff links, tie-pins & rings all sparkled against the slightest skin showing of his shirt. My father's suits were immaculate. There were so many of them... Every shirt had a corresponding tie 2 go with it. My favorite were the arrow-head style that rested just under the collar...

Matter of Fact

My Father always out dressed my Mother,
Maybe there was a secret contest going on that
we weren't aware of. She never gave me the
wink on that.

2. Only being little I closely watched Mother
getting dressed up for a night on
the town was watching leave.
That's where the Imagined Life began
A place where Eye could pretend dressup. Enter 3 part any of my own direction
a different every time but always with
similar outcomes — Eye am always
sharp & Eye always get the girl.
In my fantasy world Eye always live far away from
the public-at-large usually on a mountain
sometimes a cloud & even in an underwater
cave. (How that was accomplished was never
divulged but somehow it worked out)
Superpowers-optional but always with
secret flying abilities & Enter & exit a location
anytime Eye chose.
Hidden Places, Secret Abilities
A part of oneself that is never shown.
These & the necessary tools 4
an vibrant imagination & the main ingredients of a
good song.

3. Kiss

If not traditionally beautiful, what characteristic can a woman possess that still makes her irresistible 2 men. The answer is this — a fully functional imagination.

Laura Winnick was in possession of such a trait. No one could play act fantasies better than Laura. Not even me. Laura had a mastery of the english language that I've had never encountered b4. She could have a conversation with an imaginary friend & get everyone watching 2 suspend their belief 2 the point where they might start talking 2 the person themselves.

Laura was only five or six at the time but the only fantasy she wanted 2 play act was House. Whereas all my plays revolved around transmutation of some sort, Laura was firmly rooted in reality. It was better than television and all of her characters were happy, grounded & smart.

Out of nowhere one day Laura decided she wanted me 2 play her husband.

We weren't the 1st interracial couple in Minneapolis but we were no doubt the youngest. All lives mattered back then because race didn't. At least not in fantasy worlds of players on a dim lit theater

4. Laura kissed me 3 times that day. Each time was my 1st. The obligatory (husband on the way 2 work kiss), one when U returned, one b4 U went 2 sleep that night. Those kisses — not lasting over 3 seconds each (in line with the Hayes Code, mind U) were Everything 2 me. Laura was irritating everyday & moved her head just like the married people in the movies. 2 this day my father's rendition of the jazz standard "Laura" is one of my favorite melodies.

4. Prince

Handwriting is a lost art in need of resurrection. Everyone should have a pen pal 2 actually write 2 as often as possible. Having an audience who will not judge U opens the pen up 2 a more honest, fluid style of songwriting. My mother was also an artist so her penmanship was impeccable. She could write on blank paper and when she was finished U could C the lines of every paragraph because of how straight her pen was. She 1st showed me how 2 write my name in kindergarten. She started with my nickname Skipper & then my given name Prince.

When showing the how 2 properly write the name Prince, Eye noticed My Mother's demeanor change. She stared at the word after she wrote it the same way she stared at my father sometimes. A reverent look that she seemed 2 take pleasure in helping me own. Every school year I come kids & teachers alike would tease me about My name but it never bothered Me because it was unique. No One Else had the given name Prince except Me.

There is a technique called Visualization that was most certainly being employed back then. Even tho we had no normet its things I wrote I happen Eye would write or type. Looking back at those lists now, most everything came true. By an actual stab, at a real, fully 4med song, lists, stats were the 1st original writings. (Show lists) The list most proud of was the one containing My girlfriends. All the girls Eye liked at school were included. Whether they liked Me or not was of no consequence. Eye liked them – They were on my list so Eventually they would like me.

Rather than the cute little kid in their 1st grade class they would one day think of Me as a superstar who they really just wanna play House with.

It was His name & this was a...

The problem with Vision Quests is that they take time. Patience is required. After the encounter with Laura, who had since moved away 2 a better neighborhood, Eye needed real partners 3 explore the deeper, meaningful relationships in the subconscious world.

Eye was smaller than the rest of the kids in school so Eye needed a gimmick. Something that would make people notice me. Eye tried tapdancing at my kid sister Tyka's prodding. Tyka told me Eye was good at everything & Eye believed her. So off 2 the school talent show Eye went.

What happened next almost derailed my hopes of neighborhood stardom 4 good. After they announced my name, Eye sheepishly walked onstage & proceeded 2 do a never-changing rat-at-tat-tat step (with no music, mind u) 4 2 8½ min. which actually felt like years. until well, Eye just stopped. Eye think the applause Eye got was 4 me getting off the stage. Anything 2 make that tapping noise stop.

Dwight Buckner & his brother followed me home from school that night. 1st 2 escort my sister & Eye home because it was sundown after the talent show and secondly 2 ridicule me & my "performance". Dwight & his brother would mimic my routine in between uproarious laughter. Dwight kept saying 2 me, "What is wrong with u? Negroes ain't supposed 2 tapdance no more!"

Early on

Eye Believe Land all the power greater

When myself was at work in my life
We grew up, 1st attending 7th Day Adventist
Church where I 1st met the Andersons
Fred Anderson & His Wife Bernadette were
friends of my parents & tho Eye never asked
Eye believe now that Bernadette & my Mother
secretly had Each & their's back when it came 2 their
husbands. 4 that matter Eye feel that the Entire
planet have been maintained this very by the
feminine principal. Eye can always let my
guard down when there's a woman present.

The 1st Epileptic seizure Eye recall was when
I was about 3. Eye loved 2 play out side
& felt completely free with no ceiling. Clouds
seemed like home 2 me. One day the clouds jerked
violently spinning & Eye just remember being carried
by my Father into the living room where I came
2 on the couch. A trip 2 the hospital revealed I
was Epileptic & prone 2 seizures at any time.

My brain has always been overactive & the
blackouts would occur primarily from overthinking.

Basically bored by the poz malady (new word
alert!) of life. Eye always viewed it thru hyper-realities.

My school teacher couldn't just b the person who
taught the alphabet & math. She had 2 b a willing
participant in a mud-wrestling contest between I the

After teaching at the school. And the contest started once Eye got home after school. In the Octagon of my brain. Coming back 2 reality was always very jarring. The last seizure Eye recall happened walking 2 My Grandmother's House.

My Sister was up ahead of Me walking with my Mother. Eye just remember sitting down on the sidewalk & feeling very small as the 2 of them went farther & farther away. Eye could hear my Mother's voice calling out, "Skipper! Get up! Come On, here. Don't make come back there & carry U." Carry Me is what she had 2 do though cuz the blackout was bad. Apparently there were violent convulsions accompanying it & it scared everyone something awful. Christ imagining my Mother's true feelings about herself back then but She has the deepest Gratitude from Me 4 enduring what must have been a nightmare.

She told me that shortly after that Episode Eye approached Her & told Her that "an angel came & told Me that Eye'm not gonna be sick anymore." Eye never had another seizure.

Music is healing. Some secrets r so dark they have 2 b turned in2 song & b4 one can even begin 2 unpack them.

My mother, altho very loving & nurturing, the out going life of the party sometimes could b very stubborn & completely irrational. No One Could reason w/ the My Mother when She was in this state.

The sound of Ur parents fighting is chilling when Ur a child. If it happens 2 become physical, it can b soul crushing.

One Night Eye remember hearing them arguing & it got physical At some point My Mother crashed in my bedroom and grabbed me She was crying but managed a smile & said "tell Ur Father 2 b nice 2 me." She held me up as a buffer so that He wouldn't fight w/ Her anymore.

Things calmed down then. 4 a while. My mother subsequently got a lawyer 2 defend herself against My Father She basically wanted 2 run the household not Him. She considered Him weak & narrow minded as opposed 2 the practical man that He was. Where She wanted adventure & traveling. He just wated make sure there was food on the table.

Some topics can't be glossed over

After several breakdowns of communication
& even occasional violence My Mother &
Father divorced. Eye had no idea what
impact that would have on Me. Eye was
4 years old & more than anything just
wanted peace. A Quiet space
where Eye could hear myself think &
create. The separation was good 4
both of them at the time. They needed
2 explore themselves without
Interference from each other.
4 a time Everyone was happier. My Father
would come by Every weekend & take us 2
church & then 2 dinner afterward. Just like
b4 except now my Mother was absent. Their
stubbornness on their part would b their ultimate
undoing. Eye missed seeing Her get dressed
up in her Sunday Best. Eye missed the admiring
Eyes from the other kids cause Eye had the
most beautiful Mom. Most of all Eye missed the knowing
wink that she'd give me whenever Eye was unsure
about something. That wink meant Everything was alright.
when in fact... Everything was different now. Eye
didn't actually begin 2 know the until He left
my Mother. Being the only male in the house
with Her Eye Understood & He left.

She was 2 strong & not always in a good way. She would spend up what little $ the family had 4 survival on partying with her friends then trepass in 2 my room, "borrow" my personal $ that Eye'd gotten from babysitting local kids & then chastise me 4 even questioning her regarding the broken promise she made 2 pay me back.

In hindsight, Eye am glad Eye was able 2 help put food on the table but this was the 1st time Eye had ever had any real $ & $ it felt amazing. & made $ babysitting 4 a local celebrity D.J. named JERRY "MOTORMOUTH" MAC Hen & His dancer wife Tracy were the Ike & Tina Turner of North Minneapolis. Jerry was a God send 2 o community. Jerry was always dressed 2 the 9's. Quick-witted & Silk Smooth with the compliments & kept an xtra bankroll on hand 4 tipping. Jerry tipped everybody. If he had $ everybody had 2 have some. He loved complimenting my Mother. She "borrowed" her $ sometimes 2. Eye'm sure she never paid it back. Jerry loved Music More than anything. Whenever the latest disks would come out, Jerry would here them 1st. He belonged 2 a D.J. & Record Store Owner Pool. Having a 45 track 2 the baddest, just released jams made u top dog

in the hood. What's More Jerry had
a drum set, a piano, a mic AND
an amplifier he used 4 His D.J. Shows.
Eye had only ever seen an amplifier on TV
b4 behind The Beatles. Eye had no idea this
device would become more important 2 my life
than a store. Countless Hours Eye would spend
in Jerry's Basement looking at all the 8by10
glossies of the greatest RnB Stars. B.B. King,
Bobby Blue Bland, Al Green & Joe Tex. Jerry
even had pictures of my favorite singer James Brown
on His wall. Jerry introduced me 2 Dee
the local Record Store owner. Dee had a shop
at the End of Plymouth Ave. as we know it.
We never rode past Dee's Record Shop, without
stopping in. A trip 2 Dee's was at Happy Days.
            Any song that any of my family was
that Munched On then transcribed. Lyrics
only as Eye never learned 2 read music.
Re-Copying a lyric helps U 2 break down a line
2 C what it's made. "If U Feel like Lovin' Me,
if U've Got the Notion, Eye Second That Emotion"
Then while reading the copied lyric Eye'd learn
the chords that went with each lyric. As the
record played behind Me - Eye learned 2 play & Sing
along with every record of choice. It didn't
matter whether it was male or female - it
was the overall arrangement Eye was most
interested in.

Singing along with all records — James Brown, Ray Charles, Smokey Robinson & Aretha Franklin helps 2 develop range & a sense of soul that covers all bases. There r many great singers but that many funky singers. How a word is shaped in the mouth & the velocity or subtlety that a word is sung is what characterizes a funky singer or not.

Truly funky singers actually sound like they're singing in everyday conversation. Look at an interview with some of the greats. U know the names. If u feel like dancing while they're just talking, that's funk.

Ideally parents should stay 2gthr. The day my Mother remarried was the day Eye decided Eye wanted 2 live with my real father who loved the Bible & had a keen sense of morality & class. None of which my stepfather possessed. The best thing that could b said about him was that he made my mother happy. At 12 years of age, Eye left them 2 each other 2 go live with my father. It was the happiest day of my life. Eye could only go so far alone with no teacher. Eye needed 2 b near my hero.

New Beginnings...

The day Eye was 2 go live with my Father, there was a drop off time set... 6:00. Eye didn't know that until later... because out of spite My Mother told me she had somewhere 2 b and rushed me 2 pack so that she could drop me off some 2 hours earlier. Eye didn't care one way or another & not a single word was spoken on the 7 minute trip over 2 his apartment. My Mother pulled up, Eye got out & she left. Eye sat there emotionless at 1st then a subdued joy entered my soul. Eye knew the best was yet 2 come. Eye wanted 2 prove 2 my 1st love, My Mother Just the same Prince... My Father's stage name (now my given name) was worthy of her love, adoration & respect.

PUBERTY

R-Rated Movies at the drive-in? 4 My Step Father it was never an issue. Not only did he want 2 them, taking us a couple neighborhood kids would save him from having "the talk" with us. Not that any of us still had any disillusions about where babies came from or how they were made, but a raggedy R-Rated drive in movie in the midst of one's puberty is not the best way 2 learn about SEX.

Having the Song of Solomon read & discussed with U by someone who loves U, preferably an older would b my choice if Eye had 2 do it all over again. But We were raised by the streets. Eye did. 4 belong 2 my step father by blood so He did the best He could with the short amount of time He had. When Eye learned the foundation that stayed with Me 4 the next 2 years was after Eye reunited with my real father He said, "U got a girlfriend? Good. Don't get married & whatever U do don't get anybody pregnant. C ya when U get home." He would never take Me 2 a trashy R-rated movie. This Man Read the Bible daily and if He needed something, no matter what it was, He would make it Himself. Eye watched Him remodel & paint Rhacx Single-handedly build a Garage from scratch & fix nearly anything that had 2 do with cars, All of while holding down 2 jobs — One at HONEYWELL Manufacturing & another playing piano on downtown Mpls. Club circuit. Asking Him 2 take Me 2 C Woodstock was like going 2 the Wizard of OZ 2 ask 4 a new brain. From the trailer — watching some hippies 4 3 hours take drugs & mud baths was what He thought it was gonna Older kids who knew otherwise told it was a little of that but a WHOLE LOT of MUSIC!

After convincing the Wizard of OZ that Eye didn't need a brain, Eye really just needed more courage 2 ask him 2 take, my father smiled & said O.K. Eye'll take U on Sunday afternoon after church.

Of course that was the longest service Eye ever had 2 sit thru... Service the Black church is long 2 begin with but the thought of spending the night with Santana, Jimi Hendrix & Sly & the family stone was 2 much 2 handle. My father wanted 2 change clothes. Eye remember already standing by the car waiting 4 him crazy with anticipation. (calling back 2 mind) The whole experience reminds me 2 do the best Eye possibly can every chance Eye get 2 be on stage because somebody out there is C-ing U 4 the 1st time. Artists have the ability 2 change lives with a single performance. My father & Eye had 4 lives changed that night. The bond we cemented that very night let me know that there would always b someone in my corner when it came 2 my passion. My father understood that night what music really meant 2 me. From that moment on—he never talked down 2 me, He asked my opinion about things, He bought me my 1st guitar because we couldn't fit a piano in2 my aunt's house. The apartment We lived in was getting 2 small 4 us. So my father suggested my aunt take care of me 4 awhile.

Southside

The Northside of Mpls had 2
much testosterone 4 My taste growing up.
After Eye moved to the Southside Eye had
2 change schools. Andre Cymone who
is my same age I played bass in R band routinely in4med
me of what Eye was missing. Serious fights,
Unwanted Pregnancies, sometimes even
shootings. When a local D.J. Kyle Ray who was
much-loved in the community got killed, the
whole scene was something that Eye needed
a break from. The Southside of Mpls. was at
once another secret place that instantly set
me apart from my northside crew. Besides
that - PUBERTY hit with the strength of a hurricane
& all Eye could really think about was the opposite sex.

The cool thing is that now - Eye was in
a much more wholesome environment. My Aunt
Olivia however overly religious ... (this woman
talked about the Bible more than Jesus) loved
& cared 4 me the best she could. When it came
2 her husband Mason - on the other hand, She
was rude, highly dismissive & joyless 4 no reason ...
or so Eye thought. One day during one of my
father's weekend visits, Eye asked what had
happened & when he said, "let's go 4 a drive",
Eye knew it. Twas bout 2 go down!

We left the house & My Father's initial silence let me know that wouldn't be an ordinary talk. He told me that b4 what He was about 2 tell me, My aunt Olivia was one of the sweetest people He knew. She enjoyed homemaking & having guests over regularly 4 get 2gethers & such & she had a very robust laugh & always looked 4 a reason 2 let it out. Then one summer day she doubled back 2 the house unexpectedly 2 get her sweater. Much 2 her chagrin, she busted her husband full on with one of her friends from the church. Whether true or not - 4 me was not the issue, but it sure went a long way in explaining how one woman could b so mean 2 one man. Eye asked y they just didn't break up & He said, "Her religious faith." How & when did religion get so complicated.

Eye looked at my aunt differently after My Father broke that news 2 me. Because My uncle Mason had lost full use of His legs, He depended upon Her 4 everything. T'was like that movie Misery 'round there sometimes. Eye just spent as much time as Eye could with friends. Eye had a band over North & the fantasy combination of High School Sports & Women over South. There was a constant TUG-
of War goin' on between them. — I always.

Eventually Debbie won. There were many reasons y Eye liked Debbie. #1 on the list - Her Afro. It was perfectly round and long. When it was picked out, it didn't look like it had been stretched 2 last milli-inch 2 make it look long. It actually was long. #2 Debbie had Acne. Eye did 2 but not a bad affliction's & it made Her just vulnerable enough that She was approachable & not out of a brotha's reach. #3 She was built like a Brick House which theme song hadn't come out but we still knew what it meant. Serena Williams without the racket. One other Big Plus - She loved Music. She hipped me 2 "Draws Music": RnB primarily 4 the ladies - B4 Debbie's couldn't stomach any music without a guitar solo. Without the potential of jumpin off y would anybody, Eye thought - listen 2 Sideshow by Blue Magic & Show Me How by the Emotions Natural High by Bloodstone. Debbie's played "Show Me How" 8 times in a Row trying 2 get me 2 Kiss her on the part that says, "Eye Want 2 Kiss U Right Now." Eye finally kissed Debbie because Eye couldn't bear hearing the Emotions sing "Show Me How" 9 more times

A good ballad should always put U in the mood 4 making love.

The way Jee Emotion's lead singin' voice breaks on the words "Eye love, Eye love Eye love U Baby"... just when the end vamp is starting. Fellas, u don't need Debbie's breasts in ur hands 2 make U appreciate the value of a good ballad.

This is MY jam .... Everybody can't point 2 at least one song that is "their jam" & nobody else's. The 1st time Eye knew Eye had written of those jams was Do Me Baby. A song whose intro made me feel the same way Eye felt the 1st time Eye heard Sweet Thing by Rufus featurin Chaka Khan.

Everything about the lyric & the vocal performance is flawless. Perfect note selection on the melody but more than that - a totally believable singer and we buy every single word. Now the arrangement - the Guitar, Bass & drums make this jam. It's one of the funkiest slow songs that came out at that time. After this there were many funky ballads by Dee Ohio Players Isley Brothers Even Marvin Gaye.

If U're funky, even on a ballad U'll hear it. It's just what U R.

Trying 2 outdo the funky ballads that preceeded R work in the 80's never seemed insurmountable. Eye just figured that was then. This is now. Eye had grown in a different kind of tan. One more of mutual respect or rather than awe. U can't beat anybody that U worship. In 11th Grade Eye was standing on the "doorstep of worship." Her name was Petey. It was a nickname & something longer & strange like Patricia or something. Who knows or cares 2 remember. Petey was my exact height, weight, skin color & afro size. We were made 4 each other. Somebody 4 got 2 tell her that & she went with one of my best southside friends named Tony. Even by his own accounts, Tony was not cute. Not even remotely. 2 me he looked like a big friendly monster.

Maybe that was the attraction. Tony would carry her books as they walked down the hallway & with one look Tony would scare away anyone looking 2 nice at Petey. Heavens, she was fine, & only had one dream about Petey when Eye was sleeping but all thru 11th grade Eye dreamt her during the day. It was absolutely pathetic, & she never knew. One day in Dec. 64 the School let out 4 Xmas break Joanne & Denise - 2 of the "Fast Girls" (the ones who French Kiss better than the French) was carrying around mistletoe so they have a good excuse 2 kiss as many guys as they wanted. In No Rush 2 kiss Either one of those Rejects from the Ewww Brigade, Eye walked Extremely fast 2 my locker so Eye could get my coat & get back over North 2 Band rehearsals. By this time Debbie had left me 4 ~~THE~~ most popular dude in school—THE QUARTERBACK "4 the" School's Football Team. Of course. So unless it was Petey—Eye was better off sticking 2 my guitar. By this time Eye had purchased a vanilla Stratocaster identical 2 the one Jimi played @ Woodstock. Once Eye got 2 my locker, like a scene from a John Hughes film—the locker door closes & Petey is standing right behind it Way 2 close 4 comf~~H~~. My heart skipped a measure & then ran out ahead of me 2 go catch the school bus home. She said, with the sweetest baby-like tone—Jo Prince, what's it gonna B? Much 2 my surprise Joanne & Denise were standing right behind me both with mistletoe dangling it over my head. As Petey moved slowly closer 2 me, my heart came running back down the hallway & jumped in my chest now pumped up from courage where it belonged.

Everything that happened next was in slow-motion. Petey & Eye were kissing as if his hue knew just what the other wanted. Petey kissed me as if she had been planning this all year. It was so good Joanne started moaning & Denise had 2 stop her. "Shut up, Girl" But

Petey wouldn't stop. She grabbed my neck and started kissing Me harder. Denise said, "Dang U guys!" & then Petey stopped. She didn't let go of my neck she just stopped kissing, looked at me & said, "Did U like that?" He nodded his head YES She let go & the 3 of them started off down the down the hallway looking 4 their next victim.

On a cloud Eye left school that year more Self-assured than Eye had ever been my whole life. Eye was absolutely certain that finally Eye was living the imagined life. That wherever Eye was, Rich or Poor - all my dreams would come true.

Eye stopped at the Record Store downtown Called Music land which was like Blockbuster Video 4 Music. Dee's Record Store had long being gone & the Majors had begun the takeover. Wenly's Fast Food Burgers opened it's 1st store & Eye was just oblivious 2 it all. Petey kissed & Eye Now had in My possession Rufusized - Perhaps My favorite album by Chaka Khan 4 all the reasons stated earlier. The Piano Intro 2 packed My Bags left me with Butterflies. Eye Remember tryin 2 tell my friends How Eye felt about this music but nobody seemed 2 understand. Actually Nobody except Marcie ...

Marcie lived on the Northside.
Eye met her in total darkness at a houseparty just
like my favorite scene from the movie About Time with
Rachel McAdams. Rachel & her love interest
meet in a sensory deprivation Diner. Ur served
& dine in complete darkness. Imagine that meal.

The houseparty Eye met Marcie at wasn't
pitch black dark by choice. Nearly all
houseparties back in the day were dark inside
because disco lighting was Expensive. The
best U might do would b 2 stand by the Xmas
tree lighting so at least U could c who Ur
dancing partner might b. As Eye Recall
Eye just asked Marcie 2 dance because
She was the closest in vicinity & Eye loved
the song that had just come on. It was Skin
Tight by the Ohio Players. the bass & drums on this
record would make Stephen Hawking dance.
No disrespect - it's just that funky.

Marcie loved inner exploration as
much as Eye did. She could talk & talk & Eye
loved 2 listen because She had a speech impediment.
Her "R's" came out as "W's" as in
PWINCE & the WEVOLUTION

During these 4 plus/minus years of gettin' a band 2gether and gettin' serious money-makin' gigs, there was one guy/women who made more impact & left the impressions still being drawn upon 2day. Her name was Cari.

Cari was introduced 2 me by my estranged sister Tyko. Cari was my 1st real girlfriend. A tough, ghetto girl who personified the very thing my Father warned me against. Cari's body was criminal & her curves were most dangerous on the weekend. Cari used 2 wear Sizzlers. Infamously short Mini-Dresses with Identical Underbottoms 2 match. In the movie WATTSTAX, there's a scene of a beautiful sister wearing a sizzler dancing 2 some funk. Nothing B4 or since is colder than that sister engaging in this particular endeavor. Cari was the 1st girl 2 expose 2 both the 2 just straight-up animal lust, where rational thought is overcome by the strength of physical attraction. This feeling will draw words from the pen that one doesn't even know exist. This feeling will make one combine words that don't go 2gether but just sound good U not only read them, U can smell them.

Once a writer has actually experienced
something & oneself then they can better
tell others about it.

What happens when 2 lovers stare
at one another without speaking, so long
the separation between them disappears
& they become One. One What?

78

1.

MY MOTHER'S EYES

That's the 1st thing 👁 can remember. U know how U can tell when someone is smiling just by looking in their eyes? That was my mother's eyes. Sometimes she would squint them like she was about 2 tell U a secret. 👁 found out later my mother had a lot of secrets.

My father's piano. That's the 1st thing 👁 remember hearing. As a younger man his playing was very busy but fluid. It was a joyous sound.

The eyes & the ears of a songwriter can never get enough praise. The way things look & the way things sound, when conveyed lyrically, can give a song space & gravity.

Of course 2 this writer there was nothing more beautiful than HIs Mother's Eyes, but Y? One of the reasons is how playful they were. The fun & mischief they promised.

There were 2 Princes in the **house** where we lived. The older one with all the responsibilities of heading a household & the younger one whose only modus operandi was fun. Not just any run-of-the-mill childhood board-game fun, but fun with a wink attached. My mother liked 2 wink at Me. 👁 knew what a wink meant b4 👁 knew how 2 spell my name. A wink meant something covert was going on. Something special that only those who were in on it could attest [2]. Sometimes when my father wasn't playing piano he'd say something 2 my mother & she would wink at me.

She never told me what it meant and sometimes it would b accompanied by a gentle caress of her hand 2 my face. But 👁 am quite sure now this is the birth of my physical imagination.

An entire world of secrets & intrigue, puzzles 2 solve & good ol' fashioned make-believe. A place where everything 4 a change goes ur way. One could get used 2 this. Many artists fall down the rabbit holes of their own imaginations & never return. There have been many who decry this as self-destruction, but 👁 prefer the term FREE WILL. Life is better lived. What path one takes is what sets us apart from the rest.

My house—it was pink. It's since been knocked down. It looked like *Mad Men,* but not as nice. Simple furniture. I remember this funky energy about it. People, voices, energy. Like the Kennedys, but black. Women had hats—like Jackie. Look up black bourgeois Midwest style. Right after Ellington. Not Ellington, but the time after him. My dad's hero was Ellington. He patterned himself on him. Ellington was on top of everyone.

SEP • 64

Those considered "different" R the ones most interesting 2 us.

A vibrant imagination is where the best songs R found. Make-believe characters wearing make-believe clothes all 2gether creating memories & calling it Life.

My parents were beautiful. 2 watch them leave the crib dressed up 4 a night on the town was one of my favorite things 2 do. Even tho my mother was walking funny when she came home it was all worth [it] 2 me just 2 c them happy.

Whenever they were happy with one another all was right [in] the world.

Thinking back, my father's mood used 2 change instantly whenever my mother was dressed up.

She craved attention & He gave her plenty of it when she was sharp. Of all the family friends & relatives my parents were the sharpest! No one could accessorize like they could. My mother's jewelry, gloves & hats all had 2 match. My father's cuff linx, tie-pins & rings all sparkled within the sharkskin frame of his suit. My father's suits were immaculate. There were so many of them. . . . Every shirt had a corresponding tie 2 go with it. My favorite were the arrowhead style that rested just under the collar. . . .

Matter of fact, my father always outdressed my mother. Maybe there was a secret contest going on that we weren't aware of. She never gave me the wink on that.

OCT • 58 A

2.

I used to watch *Superman* on TV. It was the first show I had to see. I used to rush home from school to watch it. Seeing George Reeves, seeing that cape flying, him on top of buildings—I wanted that. It's funny to turn on the TV and in America you just see white people playing the heroes. People who look like the creators of the show. That affects your self-image when you're black and watching white heroes.

Only thing better than watching Mother [and] Father getting dressed up 4 a night on the town was watching them leave.

That's where the Imagined Life began. A place where 👁 could pretend dress-up & enter a fantasy of my own direction. A different storyline every time, but always with similar outcomes—👁 am always sharp & 👁 always get the girl. In my fantasy world, 👁 always live far away from the public at large, usually on a mountain, sometimes a cloud, & even in an underwater cave. (How that was accomplished was never divulged but somehow it worked out.)

Superpowers—optional but always with secret flying abilities 2 enter & exit a location anytime 👁 chose.

Hidden Places, Secret Abilities. A part of oneself that is never shown.

These r the necessary tools 4 a vibrant imagination & the main ingredients of a good song.

83

3.

KISS

If not traditionally beautiful, what characteristic can a woman possess that still makes her irresistible 2 men? The answer is this—a fully functional imagination.

Laura Winnick was in possession of such a trait. No one could play-act fantasies better than Laura. Not even me. Laura had a mastery of the English language that ☞ had never encountered b4. She could have a conversation with an imaginary friend & get everyone watching 2 suspend their [dis]belief 2 the point where they might start talking 2 the person themselves.

Laura was only five or six at the time but the only fantasy she wanted 2 play-act was House. Whereas all my plays revolved around transmutation of some sort, Laura was firmly rooted in reality. It was better than television and all of Her characters were happy, grounded, & smart.

Out of nowhere one day Laura decided she wanted me 2 play her husband.

We weren't the 1st interracial couple in Minneapolis, but we were no doubt the youngest. All lives mattered back then because race didn't. At least not in r fantasy world.

Laura kissed me three times that day. Each time was my 1st. The obligatory husband on the way 2 work kiss, one when U returned, & one b4 U went 2 sleep that night. Those kisses—not lasting over 3 seconds each, in line with the Hayes Code, mind U—were everything 2 me. Laura was initiating everything & moved her head just like the married people in the movies. 2 this day my father's rendition of the jazz standard **"Laura"** is one of my favorite melodies.

Laura looked like Elizabeth Taylor, but little. Really dark-haired.

I only found out later that my father played this very popular song called "Laura." Those sorts of coincidences amazed me. They still do.

4. PRINCE

Handwriting is a lost art in need of resurrection. Everyone should have a pen pal 2 actually write 2 as often as possible. Having an audience who will not judge U opens the pen up 2 a more honest fluid style of songwriting. My mother was also an artist, so her penmanship was impeccable. She could write on blank paper and when she was finished U could C the lines of every paragraph because of how straight her pen was. She 1st showed me how 2 write my name in kindergarten. She started with my nickname, Skipper, & then my given name, **Prince**.

When showing me how 2 properly write the name Prince, ☞ noticed my Mother's demeanor change. She stared at the word after she wrote it, the same way she stared at my father sometimes. It was his name also & this was a reverent look that she seemed 2 take pleasure in helping me own. Every school year 2 come kids & teachers alike would tease me about My name but it never bothered Me because it was unique. No One Else had the given name Prince.

Except Me.

Teachers had a problem with calling me Prince. They didn't see it as a name. They thought it wasn't fit for a name, just like King wouldn't be. So they used Skipper instead.

You know its a strange
thing, the things I dream
of that is, you and me,
to the house of our dream
I keep picturing us in it,
you in your smoking jacket
me in my lounging outfits
which I've already designed
in my mind perhaps thats
why I want you to buy
us a hi fi because theres
so many memory's so
many words in records
in thoughts that you can
put across that words
cain't reveal, Its almost
an obsession in my mind.
Our love — I want to be
a dream made into reality

        If only you could see
so deep down inside of
me. When we have each
other I feel that certain
something that I cain't
say exactly in words

with a pen in my hand. I can't put into writing either I sometimes think I could paint it in a painting — someday I plan to do that or be able to express to a painter what I feel so they can put it down in a picture for our bedroom or a very special place in our home

I would like very much for us to have dinner at the tea leaves to morrow evenning & the rest of the evenning can be of your choice. Here's what I have planned for us.

A. M. — 8:00 - 10:00 — Clean halls
                      & work etc.

~~12:00 — stay — until~~ — To be
12:30 — 2:30 = downtown Skipped to
                               Mothers
3:00 — dinner = Uncle Frank
4:30 — bed for you — until
~~9:30 — over to~~ we'll well talk
about it tomorow. good night
      Sweetheart hurry home "Mollie"

When we can plan on vacations we'll have a real nice time to gether just you and I. When you get time off like this week coming up.

It doesn't seem right telling you I love you every night so I'll have to think of something real different, that is, telling you I love you in a different way.

me →

you ←

XXXX ←
kisses

There is a technique called **Visualization** that was most certainly being employed back then, even though we had no name 4 it. Things ☙ wanted 2 happen, ☙ would write or type.

Looking back at those lists now, most everything came true. B4 an actual stab at a real, fully 4med song, lists, stats were the 1st original writings. The list [☙ was] most proud of was the one containing my girlfriends. All the girls ☙ liked at school were included. Whether they liked me or not was of no consequence. ☙ liked them—they were on my list, so eventually they would like me. Rather than the cute little kid in their 1st grade class they would one day think of Me as a superhero who they really just wanna play House with.

The problem with Vision Lists is that they take time. Patience is required. After the encounter with Laura, who had since moved away 2 a better neighborhood, ☙ needed real partners 2 explain the deeper meaningful relationships in the subconscious world.

☙ was smaller than the rest of the kids in school so ☙ needed a gimmick. Something that would make people notice me. ☙ tried tap dancing at my kid sister Tyka's prodding. **Tyka** told me ☙ was good at everything & ☙ believed her. So off 2 the school talent show ☙ went.

What happened next almost derailed my hopes of neighborhood stardom 4 good. After they announced my name, ☙ sheepishly walked onstage & proceeded 2 do a never-changing rat-a-tat step (with no music, mind U) 4 28 ½ minutes. Which actually felt like years. Until, well, ☙ just stopped. ☙ think the applause ☙ got was 4 me getting off the stage. Anything 2 make that tapping noise stop.

Dwight Buckner & his brother followed me home from school that night. 1st 2 escort my sister & ☙ home because it was sundown after the talent show and secondly 2 ridicule me & my "per4mance." Dwight & his brother would mimic my routine in between uproarious laughter. Dwight kept saying 2 me, "What's wrong with U? Negroes ain't supposed 2 tap dance no more!"

I was looking for myself outside of myself. When you're little you see yourself in other people and try to find out who you are. People say things about me like, How is his skin so light? Or, Why doesn't he age? It's because of my self-image. I don't think about myself as wrinkly. Why is your hair like that? My hair is like this because it's unadulterated. Remember that scene in *The Matrix*, where Neo is feeling the back of his neck and saying the plugs aren't there, and Morpheus says, that's your residual self-image? That's why I made lists and things. That's what I mean by visualization. I was trying to see who I would become.

Tyka looked up to me because I was like a little version of my father. She loved my father and she seemed to get under his wing. I loved both my parents, but I had a distance from my father. I still can't figure out why. Maybe because he represented discipline.

He was my neighbor. He lived up the street. We should keep his full name in there, because it's so funny. It's so Midwestern. It's like a cartoon. And we won't have anything more in there about him.

Early on I believed another power greater than myself was at work in my life. We grew up 1st attending 7th Day Adventist Church where I 1st met the Andersons. Fred Anderson and his wife, **Bernadette**, were friends of my parents, &, though I never asked, I believe now that Bernadette & my mother secretly had each other's back when it came 2 their husbands. 4 that matter I think that the entire planet has been maintained this long by the feminine principle. I can always let my guard down when there's a woman present.

The 1st epileptic seizure I recall was when I was about 3. I loved 2 play outside & felt completely free with no ceiling. Clouds seemed like home 2 me. One day the clouds started violently spinning & I just remember being carried by my father in2 the living room where I came 2 on the couch. A trip 2 the hospital revealed I was epileptic & prone 2 seizures at any time.

My **brain** has always been overactive & the blackouts would occur primarily from overthinking. Basically bred by the normalady (new word alert) of life . . . I always viewed it thru hyper-realities. My schoolteacher couldn't just b the person who taught the alphabet & math. She had 2 b a willing participant in a mud-wrestling contest between [me] & the other **teachers** at the school. And the contest started once I got home after school, in the octagon of my brain. Coming back 2 reality was always very jarring.

The last seizure I recall happened walking 2 my grandmother's house. My sister was up ahead of me, walking with my mother. I just remember sitting down on the sidewalk & feeling very small, the 2 of them went farther & farther away. I could hear my mother's voice calling out, "Skipper! Get up! Come over here. Don't make me come back there & carry U." Carry me is what she had 2 do, though, cuz *this* blackout was bad. Apparently there were violent convulsions accompanying it & it scared everyone something awful. I can't imagine my mother's true feelings about herself back then, but she has the deepest gratitude from me 4 enduring what must have been a nightmare.

She told me that shortly after that episode I approached Her & told her that an angel came & told me that I'm not gonna b sick anymore. I never had another **seizure**.

She was a big community figure. I think I'll have to add a whole chapter about her. Whenever there are documentaries about North Minneapolis, they bring her up before they bring me up. You'd asked about the feminine principle. I'd say it's that African women have an unspoken language. It's almost primordial. No one can run a village like African women. On the one hand, they're always in each other's hair—you can't keep a secret because they're talking to everyone. On the other hand, they know you need someone to survive. There's a kind of agreement: If I die you take care of my children, if you die I take care of yours. . . . It's about religion and family. It's unwavering. All birth comes from the feminine principle. Every kingdom. It's about community, not competition. When there's too much testosterone in a room, men can understand it. They'll understand why a woman goes with a man who's not in competition, who understands the feminine. It's desirable. North Minneapolis was highly competitive, a lot of testosterone. It had lost the feminine. South Minneapolis was a tightly knit community. Not competitive.

You might want to
write this in my voice.
I used to stare and
stare at everything in
the house until I was
fried. Maybe a lot of
kids do it. I'd see faces
in everything. Faces
talking to faces. I'd
stare at the marble
until I saw faces in it.
I thought, This house
is coded for me. I'd
lose myself in every
object. Good thing
there was music.
You can compare it
to the Bible, where
everything seems
coded. Place names,
especially. There's
something there,
something sacred
being guarded. Levels
of meaning. And once
you get down deep,
you can't read them
any other way.

My teacher used to
snatch kids. I'd take
her home with me [in
my mind]. She'd say
something, scold some-
one, or another kid
would scold me, and
I'd carry that with me.
I had to talk to my
mom at home or spend
time alone to get back
to zero, back to center.
I was always working
things out. If a kid gets
hit on his collarbone,
you feel the pain.

I don't often think
back to the seizures.
This was the first time
in a while [that I
thought about them].
Because I am what
I am when I am—do
you see what I mean?
I would feel vertigo
before the blackout.
Seizures—you should
research this. What's
the brain doing? A lot
of creatives have them.
And, I'm just vamping
here—but we could
use seizures as a way
of blending our voices.
Blackouts. Here comes
another blackout.

95

Peace will come when it becomes irrelevant to strike out at people. When you see that it's striking out against your own genome.

It was unusual—it was traumatic. People in the community knew. My parents never used the word with me. It was, "I'm gonna have to go away for a while." "Will you come back?" "Probably not." And this is a scene you might be better off writing: My mother used to call my father. There were late-night calls and pleas. She wanted him to come back. She'd wake my sister and me up and have us ask him to come back. And when you're asleep as a kid, you're out. It might take a while to get there, but when you do, it's REM. So when she woke me up, I felt like I was dreaming. Music would be playing. The way it worked, she'd put on breakup music, have a drink, and then make the phone call. I think that's why I can write such good breakup songs, like "Nothing Compares 2 U." I ain't heard no breakup song like I can write. The flowers are dead. [Miming receiving an urgent phone call] "Sir, the garden's dead." I have that knowledge. By the same token, love songs. No one writes love songs like I do. I play the ones that have love in them, whether they're mine or someone else's. *(cont'd)*

Music is healing. Some secrets r so dark they have 2 b turned in2 song 1st b4 one can even begin 2 unpack them.

My mother, altho very loving & nurturing, the outgoing life of the party, sometimes could b very stubborn & completely irrational. No one could reason with my mother when she was in this state.

The sound of Ur parents fighting is chilling when U're a child. If it happens 2 become **physical**, it can b soul-crushing.

One night 👁 remember hearing them arguing & it got physical. At some point my mother crashed in2 my bedroom and grabbed me. She was crying but managed a smile & said, "Tell Ur father 2 b nice 2 me." She held me up as a buffer so that he wouldn't fight with her anymore.

Things calmed down then. 4 a while. My mother subsequently got a lawyer 2 defend herself against my father. She basically wanted 2 run the household not Him. She considered him weak & narrow-minded, as opposed 2 the practical man that he was. Where she wanted adventure & traveling . . . he just wanted [2] make sure there was food on the table.

Some topics can't b glossed over. After several breakdowns of communication & even occasional violence, my Mother & Father **divorced**. 👁 had no idea what impact that would have on me. 👁 was 7 years old & more than anything 👁 just wanted peace. A quiet space where 👁 could hear myself think & create. The separation was good 4 both of them at the time. They needed 2 explore themselves without interference from each other. 4 a time everyone was happier. My father would come by every weekend & take us 2 church & then 2 dinner afterward. Just like b4 except now my mother was absent. This stubbornness on her part would b their ultimate undoing. 👁 missed seeing her get dressed up in her Sunday best. 👁 missed the admiring eyes from the other kids cause 👁 had the most beautiful mom. Most of all 👁 missed the knowing wink that she'd give me whenever 👁 was unsure about something. That wink meant everything was alright. When in fact . . . everything was different now. 👁 didn't actually begin 2 know my father until he left my mother. Being the only male in the house with Her, 👁 understood Y he left.

She was 2 strong & not always in a good way. She would spend up what little $ the family had 4 survival on partying with her friends, then trespass in2 my bedroom, "borrow" my personal $ that 👁'd gotten from babysitting local kids, & then chastise me 4 even questioning her regarding the broken promise she made 2 pay me back.

In hindsight, 👁 am glad 👁 was able 2 help put food on the table, but this was the 1st time 👁 had ever had any real $ b4 & it felt amazing. 👁 made $ babysitting 4 a local celebrity DJ named JERRY "MOTORMOUTH" MAC. Him & his dancer wife, Tracy, were the Ike & Tina Turner of North Minneapolis.

W
H
E
N
D
O
V
E
S
C
R
Y

Jerry was a godsend 2 r community. He was always dressed 2 the 9s. Quick-witted, silky smooth with the compliments, & kept an xtra bankroll on hand 4 tipping. Jerry tipped everybody. If he had $ everybody had 2 have some.

He loved complimenting my mother. She "borrowed" [his] $ sometimes 2. I'm sure she never paid it back. Jerry loved music more than anything. Whenever the latest discs would come out, Jerry would have them 1st. He belonged 2 a DJ & Record Store Owner Pool. Having a fast track 2 the baddest, just released joints made u top dog in the hood. What's more, Jerry had a drum set, a piano, a mic, AND an amplifier he used 4 his DJ shows. I had only ever seen an amplifier on TV b4 behind The Beatles. I had no idea this device would become more important 2 my life than a stove. Countless hours I would spend in Jerry's basement looking at all the 8 x 10 glossies of the greatest RnB stars, B.B. King, Bobby Blue Bland, Al Green, & Joe Tex. Jerry even had pictures of my favorite singer, James Brown, on his wall. Jerry introduced me 2 Dee, the local record store owner. Dee had a shop at the end of Plymouth Ave. as we [knew] it. We never rode past **Dee's Record Shop** without stopping in. A trip 2 Dee's was a Happy Day.

Any song that caught my fancy was 1st purchased then transcribed. Lyrics only, as I never learned 2 read music. Re-copying a lyric helps U 2 break down a line 2 c what it's made [of]. "If U feel like loving me, if U've got the notion, I Second That Emotion." Then while reading the copied lyric I'd learn the chords that went with each lyric, as the record played behind me. I learned 2 play & sing along with every record of choice. It didn't matter whether it was male or female—it was the overall arrangement I was most interested in.

Singing along with all records—James Brown, Ray Charles, Smokey Robinson, & Aretha Franklin—helps 2 develop range & a sense of soul that can cover all bases. There r many great singers but [not] that many funky singers. How a word is shaped in the mouth & the velocity or subtlety that a word is sung [with] is what characterizes a funky singer or not.

Truly funky singers actually sound like they're singing in everyday conversation. Look at an interview with some of the greats. U know the names. If U feel like dancing while they're just talking, that's funk.

(cont'd) With my parents, it was like two alphas got together and outdid each other. My mother thought there was no one cooler than Prince, my father. He had the best clothes, played the best music. She could never replicate it with someone else. Always carried a torch. I always say there's some part of your heart you should never give away. I've always lived that way. Because otherwise, I've seen it, there are times where you believe that's it. And then you close yourself off to people.

I went to Dee's when I had my first bike—an ugly, house-like bike. As soon as I had it, I was shopping at Dee's, in 1966-ish. Musicland replaced Dee's, [it was] a big corporate chain. Put Dee's out of business. It's all about competition, how can we outsell. Monkeys and primates could sell music. With Clear Channel [a radio and media conglomerate, since rebranded as iHeartMedia] it becomes like *Soylent Green*—people feeding people to people. We need to tell them that they keep trying to ram Katy Perry and Ed Sheeran down our throats and we don't like it no matter how many times they play it.

In 1967 or '68, my mother remarried Hayward Baker, from Chicago—they got married there.

Ideally parents should stay 2gether. The day my mother **remarried** was the day ☞ decided ☞ wanted 2 live with my real father, who loved the Bible & had a keen sense of morality & class. None of which my stepfather possessed. The best thing that can b said about him was that he made my mother happy. At 12 years of age, ☞ left them 2 each other 2 go live with my father. It was the Happiest Day of My Life. ☞ could only go so far alone with no teacher. ☞ needed 2 b near my hero.

Skipper Nelson Baker
2620 8th Ave. North
Mpls., Minnesota
55400

HEMPSTEAD, NY
PM
2 JAN
1971

FRANKLIN D. ROOSEVELT
U.S. POSTAGE
6¢

5. NEW BEGIN- NINGS

I think my father was kind of lashing out at my mother when he named me Prince. I was into [music] a little too much for her. . . . She didn't like that because music is what broke up her marriage. My father was too serious about music. I was considered strange. I recall having a lot of strange dreams. I spent a lot of time alone. I turned to music. In some ways it was more important than people. (*Los Angeles Times*, 1980)

The day 👁 was 2 go live with my father, there was a drop-off time set . . . 6:00. 👁 didn't know that until later . . . because out of spite My Mother told me she had somewhere 2 b and rushed me 2 pack so that she could drop me off some 2 hours earlier. 👁 didn't care one way or another & not a single word was spoken on the 12-minute trip over 2 his apartment. My mother pulled up, 👁 got out & she left. 👁 sat there emotion-less at 1st, then a subdued joy entered my soul. 👁 knew the best was yet 2 come. 👁 wanted 2 prove 2 my 1st love, my mother, that the name **Prince** . . . my father's stage name & now my given name, was worthy of her love, adoration, & respect.

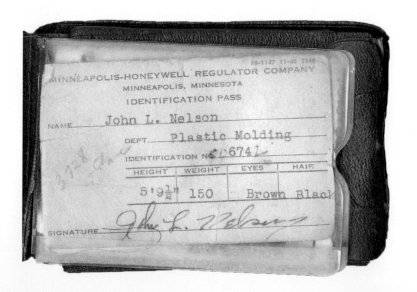

6. PUBERTY

Once my mother re-married, it was during the time period in my life where she had to teach me about the birds and the bees. And I've never asked her about this, but I think there was some sort of plan to initiate me heavy and quick. I was given *Playboy* magazine, and there was erotic literature laying around. It was very easily picked up. It was pretty heavy at the time. I think it really affected my sexuality a great deal. (To Chris Rock on *VH1 to One,* 1997)

Religion is about self-development. That's all it is.

R-rated movies at the drive-in? 4 my stepfather it was never an issue. Not only did he want 2 c them, taking U & a couple neighborhood kids would save him from having **"The Talk"** with us.

Not that any of us still had any disillusions about where babies came from or how they were made, but a raggedy R-rated drive-in movie in the midst of one's puberty is not the best way 2 learn about SEX.

Having the Song of Solomon read & discussed with U by someone who loves U, preferably an [elder], would b my choice if ☞ had 2 do it all over again. But we were raised by the streets. ☞ didn't belong 2 my stepfather by blood so he did the best he could with the short amount of time he had. When ☞ learned the foundation that stayed with me 4 the next 25 years was after ☞ reunited with my real father. He said, "U got a girlfriend? Good. Don't get married & whatever U do don't get anybody pregnant. Cya when U get home." He would never take me 2 a trashy R-rated movie. This man read the Bible daily.

And if **he** needed something, no matter what it was, he would make it himself. ☞ watched him remodel & paint R house, singlehandedly build a garage from scratch & fix nearly anything that had 2 do with cars. All of [this] while holding down 2 jobs—one at Honeywell Manufacturing & another playing piano on [the] downtown Mpls. Club circuit. Asking him 2 take me 2 c Woodstock was like going 2 the Wizard of Oz 2 ask 4 a new brain. From the trailer—watching some hippies 4 3 hours take drugs & mud baths was what he thought it was gonna [be]. Older kids who knew otherwise told [me] it was a little of that but a WHOLE LOT of MUSIC!

A Whole New Concept In Music
with the

PRINCE ROGERS TRIO

New Sounds!

New Music!

Featuring

- No One Else
- Spinning Wheel Blues
- Seventh Ave. Express
- How Come
- Blue Skirt Waltz
- One Kiss
- One Night of Love
- It's A Sin To Tell A Lie
- Red Sails In The Sunset
- September Song
- Deep Purple

- Laura
- I Wish You Love
- Blue Moon
- I Wonder What Became of Sally
- Sweet Sixteen
- Alice Blue Gown
- Irish Eyes Are Smiling
- Sentimental Journey
- Night Train
- Red Top

MANY, MANY MORE!

PRINCE ROGERS
PIANO

3728 FIFTH AVENUE SOUTH
MINNEAPOLIS 9, MINN.   PLEASANT 3046

915 LOGAN NORTH   MINNEAPOLIS

PRINCE ROGERS
A WHOLE NEW CONCEPT IN MUSIC

374-5764   MUSIC For All Occasions

After convincing the Wizard of Oz that 👁 didn't need a brain, 👁 really just needed more courage 2 ask him 2 take [me], my father smiled and said OK. 👁'll take U on Sunday afternoon after church.

Of course that was the longest service 👁 ever had 2 sit thru. . . . Service [in] the black church is long 2 begin with, but the thought of spending the night with Santana, Jimi Hendrix, & Sly & the Family Stone was 2 much 2 handle. My father wanted 2 change clothes. 👁 remember already standing by the car waiting 4 him, crazy with anticipation. Calling back 2 mind the whole experience reminds me 2 do the best 👁 possibly can every chance 👁 get 2 b onstage because somebody out there is c-ing U 4 the 1st time. Artists have the ability 2 change lives with a single per4mance. My father & 👁 had R lives changed that night. The bond we cemented that very night let me know that there would always b someone in my corner when it came 2 my passion. My father understood that night what music really meant 2 me. From that moment on—he never talked down 2 me. He asked my opinion about things. He bought me my 1st guitar because we couldn't fit a piano in2 my aunt's house. The apartment we lived in was getting 2 small 4 us. So my father suggested my aunt take care of me 4 a while.

4th QUARTER MID-TERM PROGRESS REPORT

Student _Prince Nelson_   Class _English_   Period _4_

Times absent from class ___1___   Times tardy to class ___0___   Homeroom _213_

PRESENT STANDING

Quantity of Work	Quality of Work
____ completed more than required work	X above average
____ completed all required work	____ average
____ completed most required work	____ below average
X completed only some required work	
____ completed little required work	

Prince could be doing much better work than he is, even though it is already above average. He has fine skills and a clever, perceptive mind.

The following behaviors are those that can help a student achieve the class goals and make the class a good learning place:

Your student generally........

	YES	NO	DOES NOT APPLY
Comes to class on time.....................	X		
Brings necessary work materials...........		X	
Is a good listener when teacher or other students are talking.............		X	
Pays attention to instructions............		X	
Completes assignments in class...........		X	
Makes up missed work.....................			X
Treats other people with consideration....	X		
Willingly accepts a challenge and looks for new ones.........................		X	
Participates in class discussion.........	X		
Often gives aid or help to teacher and other students........................		X	

_____

_____

SUGGESTED REMEDIAL MEASURES

____ come to class	____ complete homework on time
____ come to class on time	____ study for tests
____ make up work promptly	____ ask for help when needed
X pay attention in class	_____
X complete assignments in class	_____
X bring work materials	_____

If you would like further information, please call Bryant Jr. High at 822-3161. Leave a message for me and I will return your call. If you would like to write comments, please do so on the back and return this sheet to me. Thank you.

Mrs. Hoben
(Teacher)

108

7. SOUTH-SIDE

A local DJ is like a vortex of energy. DJs should bring communities together. The president should be like a local DJ.

The Northside of Mpls. had 2 much testosterone 4 my taste growing up. After ☞ moved 2 the Southside ☞ had 2 change schools. André Cymone, who is my same age & played bass in R band, routinely in4med me of what ☞ was missing. Serious fights, unwanted pregnancies, sometimes even shootings. When a **local DJ**, Kyle Ray, [who] was much-loved in the community got killed, the whole scene was something that ☞ needed a break from. The Southside of Mpls. was at once another secret place that instantly set me apart from my Northside crew. Besides that, PUBERTY hit with the strength of a hurricane & all ☞ could really think about was the opposite sex.

The cool thing is that now ☞ was in a much more whole-some environment. My aunt Olivia, however overly religious (this woman talked about the Bible more than Jesus), loved & cared 4 me the best she could. When it came 2 her husband, Mason, on the other hand, she was rude, highly dismissive & joyless 4 no reason . . . or so ☞ thought. One day during one of my father's Weekend Visits, ☞ asked what had happened, & when he said, "Let's go 4 [a] drive," ☞ knew it[.] T'was about 2 go down!

We left the house & my father's initial silence let me know that [this] wouldn't b an ordinary talk. He told me that b4 what he was about 2 tell me, my aunt Olivia was one of the sweetest people he knew. She enjoyed homemaking & having guests over regularly 4 get 2gethers & such. & she had a very robust laugh & always looked 4 a reason 2 let it out. Then one summer day she doubled back 2 the house unexpectedly 2 get her sweater. Much 2 her chagrin, she busted her husband full-on with one of her friends from the church. Whether true or not—4 me [this] was not [the] issue, but it sure went a long way in explaining how one woman could b so mean 2 one man. ☙ asked y they just didn't break up & he said, "Her religious faith." How, Y, & when did religion get so complicated?

☙ looked at my aunt differently after my father broke that news 2 me. Because my uncle Mason had lost full use of his legs, he depended upon her 4 everything. T'was like that movie *Misery* 'round there sometimes. ☙ just spent as much time as ☙ could with friends. ☙ had a band over North & the fantasy combination of High School Sports & Women over South. There was a constant Tug of War goin' on between the 2 always.

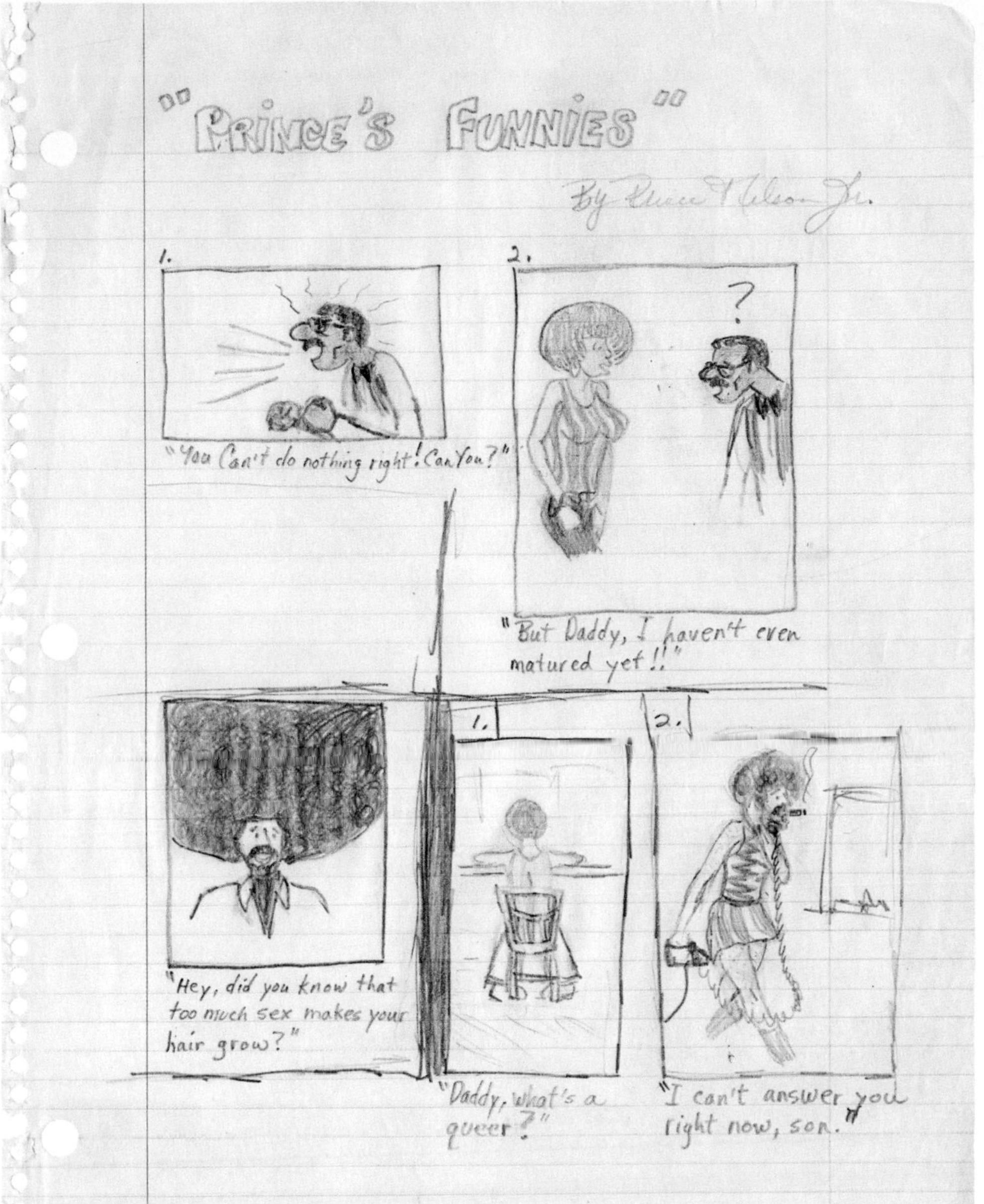

"Prince's Funnies"

By Prince Nelson Jr.

1. "You can't do nothing right! Can you?"

2. "But Daddy, I haven't even matured yet!!"

"Hey, did you know that too much sex makes your hair grow?"

1. "Daddy, what's a queer?"

2. "I can't answer you right now, son."

111

Eventually Debbie won. There were many reasons y 👁 liked **Debbie**. #1 on the list—her afro. It was perfectly round and long. When it was picked out it didn't look like it had been stretched 2 [the] last milli-inch 2 make it look long. It actually was long. #2, Debbie had acne. 👁 did 2, but not as bad as hers, & it made her just vulnerable enough that she was approachable & not out of a brotha's reach. #3, She was built like a Brick House, which theme song hadn't come out but we knew what it meant. Serena Williams without the racket. One other Big Plus, she loved music. She hipped me 2 "Draws Music," RnB primarily 4 the ladies—b4 Debbie, 👁 couldn't stomach any music without a guitar solo. Without the potential of jumping off Y would anybody, 👁 thought, listen 2 "Sideshow" by Blue Magic, "Show Me How" by the Emotions, [or] "Natural High" by Bloodstone? Debbie played "Show Me How" 8 times in a row trying 2 get me 2 kiss her on the part that says, "👁 want 2 kiss U right now." 👁 finally kissed Debbie because 👁 couldn't bear hearing the Emotions sing "Show Me How" 9 more times.

A good ballad should always put U in the mood 4 making love. The way the Emotions' lead singer's voice breaks on the words "👁 love, 👁 love, 👁 love U baby . . ." just when the end vamp is starting. Fellas, U don't need Debbie's breasts in Ur hands 2 make U appreciate the value of a good ballad.

I'm not sure about this section. Debbie taught me about black women and their love of soul music. And how they heard it. It was right when I was getting my first band together. Debbie was a cheerleader. Like Serena Williams as a cheerleader, if you can picture that. She left me for the high school quarterback. Big, good-looking guy who, even then, could throw the ball down the field. I couldn't be the quarterback at school, so I quarterbacked my band. And I should get into that—I'll write on that. I was thirteen years old and I could see everything, literally. Everything is self-creation. I am my father. I am the leader of the band. It's an alpha thing. When you get two alphas together, like me and Lenny Kravitz, who can also play all the instruments, I don't have to say, hey we should do it this way. It'll be like he plays drums, I play bass, or he plays bass, I play drums, and then we both play guitar and in twenty minutes we have a track. Michael [Jackson] was an alpha. He wasn't the oldest brother, but they all listened to him. And when he finally went solo . . . [imitates an explosion] Same with Beyoncé. People attack her for the way she talks to her band, but she knows what she wants. She's creating. The Bible says that when you find a leader like that, as a society, you should let them step back and [you should] listen. We might need to invent a new word for it.

With that song, I took the R&B ballad form I'm talking about here and updated it for the eighties.

This is my jam. . . . Everybody can point 2 at least one song that is "their jam" & nobody else's. The 1st time 👁 knew 👁 had written [one] of those jams was "**Do Me, Baby,**" a song whose intro made me feel the same way 👁 felt the 1st time 👁 heard "Sweet Thing" by Rufus featuring Chaka Khan.

Everything about the lyric & the vocal per4mance is flawless. Perfect note selection on the melody but more than that—a totally believable singer and we buy every single word. Now the arrangement—the guitar, bass, & drums make this jam. It's one of the funkiest slow songs that came out at that time. After this there were many funky ballads by the Ohio Players, Isley Brothers & even Marvin Gaye.

If U're **funky**, even on a ballad U'll hear it. It's just what U R.

Trying 2 outdo the funky ballads that preceded R work in the '80s never seemed insurmountable. 👁 just figured that was then, this is now. 👁 had grown in2 a different kind of fan. One more of mutual respect rather than awe. U can't beat anybody that U worship. In 11th grade "👁 was standing on the doorstep of worship." Her name was Petey. It was a nickname 4 something longer & strange like Patricia or something. Who knows or cares 2 remember. Petey was my exact height, weight, skin color, & afro size. We were made 4 each other. Somebody 4got 2 tell her that & she went with one of my best Southside friends named Tony. Even by his own accounts, Tony was not cute. Not even remotely. 2 me, he looked like a big, friendly monster!

Maybe that was the attraction. Tony would carry her books as they walked down the hallway & with one look Tony would scare away anyone looking 2wice at Petey. Heavens, she was Fine. 👁 only had one dream about Petey when 👁 was sleeping, but all thru 11th grade 👁 dreamt [of] her during the day. It was absolutely pathetic & she never knew. One day in Dec. b4 the school let out 4 Xmas break, Joanne & Denise—2 of the "Fast Girls" (the ones who French kiss better than the French)—[were] carrying around mistletoe so they [had] a good excuse 2 kiss as many guys as they wanted. In no rush 2 kiss either one of those rejects from the Ewww Brigade, 👁 walked extremely fast 2 my locker so 👁 could get my coat & get back over North 2 band rehearsals. By this time Debbie had left me 4 the most popular dude in school—THE QUARTERBACK 4 the school's football team. Of course. So unless it was Petey, 👁 was better off sticking 2 my guitar. By this time 👁 had purchased a vanilla Stratocaster identical 2 the one Jimi played [at] Woodstock. Once 👁 get 2 my locker, like a scene from a John Hughes film, the locker door closes & Petey is standing right behind it, way 2 close 4 com4t. My heart skipped a measure & then ran out ahead of me 2 go catch the school bus home. She said, with the sweetest baby-like tone, "So, Prince, what's it gonna B?" Much 2 my surprise, Joanne & Denise were standing right behind me, both with mistletoe, dangling it over my head. As Petey moved slowly closer 2 me, my heart came running back down the hallway & jumped in my chest, now pumped up from courage, where it belonged.

Everything that happened next was in slow motion. Petey & 👁 were kissing as tho we knew just what the other wanted. Petey kissed me as if she had been planning this all year. It was so good, Joanne started moaning & Denise had 2 stop her. "Shut up, girl."

Rhythm came from Africa. We need to stop frontin' about that. Rhythm and heartbeats.

Marcie + Prince

Petey wouldn't stop. She grabbed my neck and started kissing me harder. Denise said, "Dang, U guys!" & then Petey stopped. She didn't let go of my neck, she just stopped kissing, looked at me & said, "Did U like that?" He nodded his head YES. She let go & the 3 of them started off down the hallway looking 4 their next victim.

On a cloud ☜ left school that year more self-assured than ☜ had ever been my whole life. ☜ was absolutely certain that finally ☜ was living the imagined life. That wherever ☜ was, rich or poor—all my **dreams** would come true.

If I want this book to be about one overarching thing, it's freedom. And the freedom to create autonomously. Without anyone telling you what to do or how or why. Our conscious- ness is programmed. We see things a certain way from a young age—we're rogrammed to keep doing them that way. Then you have to spend adult- hood learning how to overcome it, to read out the programs. Try to create. I want to tell people to create. Just start by creating your day. Then create your life.

☜ stopped at the record store downtown called Musicland, which was like Blockbuster Video 4 music. Dee's Record Store had long been gone & the majors had begun the takeover. Wendy's fast food burgers opened its 1st store & ☜ was just oblivious 2 it all. Petey kissed [me] & ☜ now had in my possession *Rufusized*—perhaps my favorite album by Chaka Khan 4 all the reasons stated earlier. The piano intro 2 "Pack'd My Bags" left me with butterflies. ☜ remember trying 2 tell my friends how ☜ felt about this music but nobody seemed 2 understand. Actually nobody except Marcie . . .

Marcie lived on the Northside.

☜ met her in total darkness at a house party just like my favorite scene from the movie *About Time* with Rachel McAdams. Rachel & her love interest meet in a sensory deprivation Diner. U R served & dine in complete darkness. Imagine that meal.

The house party ☜ met Marcie at wasn't pitch black by choice. Nearly all house parties back in the day were dark inside because disco lighting was expensive. The best U might do would b 2 stand by the Xmas tree lighting so at least U could C who Ur dancing partner might b. As ☜ recall ☜ just asked Marcie 2 dance because she was the closest in [the] vicinity & ☜ loved the song that had just come on. It was "Skin Tight" by the Ohio Players & the bass & drums on this record would make Stephen Hawking dance. No disrespect—it's just that funky.

Marcie loved inner exploration as much as ☜ did. She could talk & talk & ☜ loved 2 listen because she had a speech impediment. Her *R*s came out as *W*s, as in PWINCE & THE WEVOLUTION.

During these 4mative years of getting r band 2gether and getting serious money-making gigs, there was one young woman who made more impact & left the impressions still being drawn upon 2day. Her name was Cari.

Introduced 2 me by my estranged sister Tyka, Cari was my 1st real girlfriend. A tough ghetto girl who personified the very thing my father warned me against: Cari's body was criminal & her curves were most dangerous on the weekend. Cari used 2 wear sizzlers, infamously short minidresses with identical underbottoms 2 match. In the movie *Wattstax,* there's a scene of

a beautiful sister wearing a sizzler, dancing 2 some funk. Nothing b4 or since is colder than that sister engaging in this particular endeavor. Cari was the 1st girl 2 expose a brotha 2 just straight-up animal lust. Where rational thought is overcome by the strength of physical attraction. This feeling will draw words from the pen that one doesn't even know exist. This feeling will make one combine words that don't go 2gether but just sound so good U not only read them, U can smell them.

Once a writer has actually experienced something 4 oneself, then they can better tell others about it.

What happens when 2 lovers stare at one another without speaking so long the separation between them disappears & they become one. One What?

PART II.

FOR
YOU

{ PHOTO BOOK~

BORN: Dec. 19th, 1977

TIME: 3:00 a.m.

PLACE: 653 Redwood Ave. Corte Madera, California

MOTHER and FATHER: Me, Prince

UP UNTIL PAGE 11 NATIONALITY: 11 Blacks, 4 Whites, 3 Mulattos and 1 Italian. (THAT MEANS THAT BLACKS ARE NO LONGER A HA, HA, HA, HA, ... MINORITY.)

REASON FOR BIRTH: Didn't have nothing better to do. Plus, I couldn't go to sleep.

WEIGHT: Pretty light.

HEIGHT: Tall as Sherman

FAVORITE PHOTO: That one ——————————————→

REASON: 'CAUSE I GOT A LOTTA POSTAGE STAMPS LICKED THAT DAY.

DELIVERY: Fairly easy

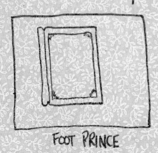

FOOT PRINCE

HAND PRINCE

I HAVE TO STOP WRITING. THIS PAPER IS GIVING ME HAY FEVER! AAAHHCHOO!

MY

FIRST

CAR!

CUTE,

HUH?

MY
"MANAGER"
OWEN.
COULD THIS BE
WHY I'M
BROKE?

THE TALKING
FLY
AND HIS
TRAINER,
MISS

PICKUPANDBOOK

CYKA and ANDRE

"FIRST
CAR
WASH"

"SHUT
UP!"

EDDIE
AND
SANCHEZE

OWEN— PREPARING FOR
A VERY IMPORTANT
MEETING WITH
MO OSTIN.
(President of Warner Bros.)

"I USUALLY BRING
MY TEETH TO THE
STUDIO"

THE WIND DOES
GREAT THINGS FOR
ONE'S HAIR!

VIEW FROM THE
CELL I WAS IN
WHEN I SIGNED
MY 1st
RECORD
CONTRACT.

"PEE-PEE
IS
NOT A
BAD
WORD."
(ANDRE'S
MOTHER,
BERNADETTE)

"FOX
STROLLING
DOWN
A
BLOCK
IN
L.A."

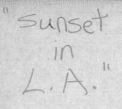
"Sunset in L.A."

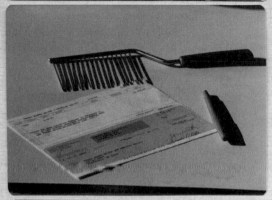

"MY FIRST CHECK FROM THE COMPANY"

VIEW FROM THE SHERATON UNIVERSal HOTEl

"HEY,
WHAT'S
HAPPENING?!"

← BAD
DAD

"HIT ME IN
THE CHEST!
GO AHEAD,
TAKE YOUR
BEST
SHOT!"

?

"THE
LAWN
AND
ROBIN
CROCKETT"

(my cousin Deniece)

TOMMY, IN HIS
USUAL
POSITION
(TOMMY VICARI - ENGINN-
NNNEERED MY 1st
ALBUM)

' THIS
BROAD
COULD STOP
TRAFFIC '

KISS ME, C'MON
I DARE YOU!

NO, THIS NOT
A
POSTCARD!

"I MUST PROVE
TO THE WORLD
THAT BLIND
PEOPLE CAN
PLAY
TENNIS
TOO!"

MY FIRST
MONEY-PAYING
GIG"
WAS DONE HERE.
CAPACITY CROWD
OF 113 CAME.
BOY, WAS IT
WET.

2 PAGES
LATER,
STILL
THERE!
YES, THERE'S
SLEEP IN YOUR
EYES!

"PWINCE!"

100

Marcie
Dixon

"My... shrink... says... I'm not getting enough silicone."

98

BEFORE...

... and after the operation

"my
First
House"

Yellow?

"Now's as good
a time as
any to learn
to ride
this mug.

DAD

Sausalito

View from front
yard at house
in L.A.

2810 Montcalm
Hollywood

"♪♪ It's impossible ♪♪
to stick a
caddillac
♪ up your, ♪♪
nose."
(The Brothers Funk)
David R.
&
Owen

Venice,
Califorly

Pictured with cane
is
Thomas Edison

"I GOT FIVE HITS!"

Pepe &Willie

"Why don'tcha come up and see me and the dog sometimes"

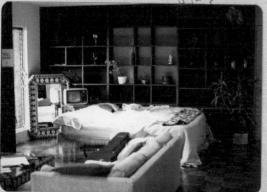

The bumproom in L.A.

"Are you sure groupies get their start like this?"
"Don't bite off your tongue when you snap the picture."

Don't worry!
I've seen better faces on an Iodine bottle!

2810 Montcalm
Andre in window
Tommy
& Diane
is
right dare →

By the time I was a sophomore, school had gotten to be a real drag. I was getting further and further into making music. The more I found myself entertaining at local gigs during the night, the more I hated the thought of going to school in the morning.

But later on, there I was, seventeen, a graduate and still frustrated. I felt that I had to keep going after the music but didn't know how long I'd be able to do it and eat, too. I did know that I wanted something more than nine to five.

(*Insider,* 1978)

This is a crazy crazy snapshot of me in Venice.

FOXPRINT
FOX PHOTO
®
JAN '78   TLA   JAN '78

FOXPRINT
FOX PHOTO
®
TLA   JAN '7

This is the terrace outside my bedroom. I sit out here and think, sometimes.

This is my bedroom.

Notice: I still don't
make my bed.

llllll

Another shot of my bedroom. There's the little amp you bought for me on the chair.

back then, because there's so many people around me now. I wrote a lot of sexual songs back then, but they were mainly things that I wanted to go on, not things that *were* going on. Which is different from what I write about now. (*Musician,* 1983)

I had originally gone to New York, and I got two offers when I came out [there] to live with my sister. The only problem there was I didn't have a cat in there fighting for me, to get me artistic control over the production end of it. (*New York Rocker,* 1981)

The only way I can relate to that period,
is that it was part of a search. . . . While
I was living with [my sister] Sharon I got
hooked up with a woman producer who
was always busy pitching her own angles.
She was only looking at me as a singer.
The kind that opts for the silk capes,
high-heeled shoes, and white Cadillacs.
You know, somebody who dresses and
sings the same part—a nice dresser and
a sweet singer. I tried to explain that
even though I didn't have the key to the
recording industry, that I knew myself,
and that I knew for sure what I would
and wouldn't do for that key. I told her
I never considered myself a singer. I saw
myself as an instrumentalist who started
singing out of necessity. I don't think
I ever got through, but I tried explaining—
that to me, my voice is just like one of
the instruments I play. It's just one thing
I do. (*Insider,* 1978)

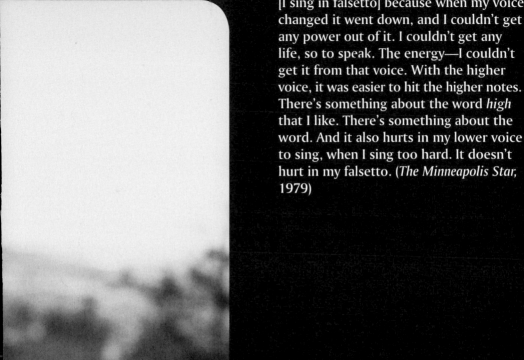

[I sing in falsetto] because when my voice changed it went down, and I couldn't get any power out of it. I couldn't get any life, so to speak. The energy—I couldn't get it from that voice. With the higher voice, it was easier to hit the higher notes. There's something about the word *high* that I like. There's something about the word. And it also hurts in my lower voice to sing, when I sing too hard. It doesn't hurt in my falsetto. (*The Minneapolis Star*, 1979)

When I got back to Minneapolis, that's
when I first met Owen Husney. I had
been talking to him over the phone. . . .
And he wanted to manage an act. The
main thing he said was that no one
should produce a record of mine—
I should do it. . . . Owen believed in me,
he really did. First of all, nobody believed
I could play all the instruments. . . .
Well, I got a couple offers and the only
difference between Warner Bros. and
the others was that they [Warner] didn't
want to let me do production, they
didn't want to let me plan anything
on the records. (*Musician,* 1983)

I'm very stubborn, real bullheaded. If I want something, I really fight for it. If I really believe in it. The first album— I really believed that I should produce it. They—the people in power—tried to put me in with what was the happening sound, the few cats on top. I wanted to get away from that. So, I put out "Soft and Wet," and that was OK. Nobody else was doing that. (*Ebony,* 1986)

No. 3590

DATE
12-30-77
CUSTOMER'S ORDER
SALESMAN
TERMS
F. O. B.
VIA

Sold To _Owen Husney_
653 Redwood Ave.
Corte Madera, Ca. 94925

Shipped To _____

Address _____

Polymoog synthesizer rental
for PRINCE

Dec. 19 and 20 @ $50/day $100 00

check to: Shirley Walker
323 Strand Ave.
Pleasant Hill, Ca. 94523
soc. sec. # 545-74-4950

Owen:
I will send you the repair bill for
reloading the keys. The note that went out is
covered on warrenty. Good luck with the album.
Hope it goes Platinum in the 1st week.

7H 737 Rediform   ● I N V O I C E ●

I wanted to make a different-sounding
record. We originally planned to use horns,
but it's really hard to sound different if
you use the same instruments. By not
using horns on this record, I could make
an album that would sound different
right away. So I created a different kind
of horn section by multi-tracking a
synthesizer and some guitar lines.

I think the main reason artists fall when they try to play all of the instruments is because, either they can't play all the instruments really well—there is usually a flaw somewhere—or they don't play with the same intensity each track. It's a hard project to do, but you have to pretend each time that this is going to be your only track and that you're the only guy who's going to play that instrument. So every time you go into the recording booth, you have to play like it's your only shot. If you do that, what you end up with is a whole band that is playing with the same intensity. (*The Minneapolis Tribune*, 1978)

SOFT -n- WET   by Percy

Hey, lover... I've got a sugar cane
That I wanna lose in you, baby, can you stand the pain?
Hey, lover... baby, don't you see?
There's so many things that you do to me.
  (Oooo Baby)
All I wanna see is the love in your eyes.
All I wanna hear is your sweet love sighs.
& All I wanna feel is your burning flame.
Tell me, tell me baby that you feel the same.
(Tell me, that you feel the same way I do. Tell me that you love
  me, girl)

If this is lust, then I must confess, I feel it every day.
If this is wrong, then I long to be as far from right as
I may... Soft -n- Wet, Soft-n- Wet...!

Everytime I'm with you, you just love me to death.
Oooo Wee Baby, You leave me without... breath!
(Oooo baby)
                    OVER ⟹

I was always trying to get [the band] to
do something different, and I was always
teamed up on for that. Like, in an argument
or something like that, or a fight, or
whatever . . . it was always me against
them. That's when I wrote "Soft and
Wet," which was the first single I put out.
I really liked the tune, but everyone
thought it was filthy, and "you didn't
have no business doing stuff without us,
anyway." I just did what I wanted to.
And that was it. (*Musician*, 1983)

SOFT-n-WET

You're just as soft as a lion tamed and
You're just as wet as the evening rain.
I really dig it when you call my name
Your love is driving me, You're driving me insane.

Crazy baby, Oooo girl. Crazy 'bout your love

Soft-n-Wet   You are...
Soft-n-wet   Your love is...
Soft-n-wet   Oooo———
"Soft-n-wet"

THE END

SOFT & WET

ANGORA FUR. THE AEGEAN SEA
IT'S A SOFT, WET LOVE THAT YOU HAVE FOR ME
BEYOND THE STARS, BENEATH THE SEA
THERE'S SO MANY THINGS THAT YOU DO TO ME ●

ALL I WANT TO SEE IS THE LOVE IN YOUR EYES
ALL I WANT TO HEAR IS YOUR SWEET LOVE SIGHS
I'm HIT WITH THE ARROW AND FEELING THE PAIN
TELL ME, TELL ME, TELL ME THAT YOU FEEL THE SAME

IF THIS IS LUST, THEN I MUST CONFESS I FEEL IT
EVERYDAY IF THIS IS WRONG, THEN I LONG TO BE
AS FAR FROM RIGHT AS I MAY.

EVERYTIME I'm WITH YOU, YOU JUST LOVE ME
TO DEATH, OOO WEE BABY, LEAVE ME WITHOUT
BREATH!

YOU'RE JUST AS SOFT AS A LION TAMED &
YOU'RE JUST AS WET AS THE EVENING RAIN &
I REALLY DIG IT WHEN YOU CALL MY NAME,
YOUR LOVE IS DRIVING ME, YOU'RE DRIVING ME
INSANE. CRAZY, BABY! & CRAZY 'BOUT
YOUR

SOFT & WET — 8 times
END ON 9

Side One "Prince / For You"
1. For You (P. Nelson)
2. Bodyfreeze (P. Nelson)
3. Never Really Fell Out Of Love With You (P. Nelson)
4. You Are Everything To Me (P. Nelson)
5. I Spend My Time Loving You (P. Nelson)

Side Two
1. Soft and Wet (C. Moon / P. Nelson)
2. Baby (P. Nelson)
3. Let Me Touch You (P. Nelson)
4. Love In The Morning (P. Nelson)
5. Send In The Clowns (J. Collins)

612-871-6200: Owen Husne
Warner Bros.
A & M
Columbia

Dave Rivkin - home - 827-6597

PRINCE...

"" 18-year-old Producer, Arranger, Songwriter and only performer on a magnificent debut album from Warner Bros. Records...

PRINCE ~ FOR YOU

Personal Management:
Owen R. Husney/American Artists
4450 ~~~~~
~~~~~ ~~~~~ Salon

"Baby" — continued vocal harmonies
(Chorus at end)

chorus:

turnover: 1. tape notes
2. harmony from E (lower harmony)
3. higher harmony from B
4. low mult to B
5. mult lead on climax high note

verse: same as 2nd verse
3rd

last
middle: 1. tape notes = F# to Ab vibrato on 2nd note
2. A to B vibrato on 2nd note (higher harmony)
3. lower harmony = B to Db
4. same as 1st middle
5. same as 1st middle

last
turnover: same as ⅘ turnover above

chorus: 1. tape notes
2. higher harmony for 1
3. harmony higher for 2 just on ah mult 2 on "Baby"
4. Lower harmony than tape notes
5. Lower harmony than 4

end: 1. mult to lead
2. A scale (ascending to 9th degree harmony on "just like your
3. 3rd degree scale (" " " ") harmony " " " "
4. 5th " " (" " " ") echo just like yours
5. Echo just like yours echo ju

HELLO

Baby ReMix #1

Written by
Bianca Jagger
& Chaka Khan

Timeline

DDL 120ms

Delay
Delay 15¼

BROTHER, TOMMY

Rec Bass Pianno Pianno Dr S Dr Kick Are Double Other Other Other La La Lessa Rec Rev Snys Snys Snys Guit Guit Guit
Piano 2P Float@ B.5 Effect 2 1 3 Vac Vac Jay Rev Rev
@3f 90 020 5 Vione
25 @25 @25
2P

1 2 3 4 5 6 7 8 9 10 11 12 13 14 15 16 17 18 19 20 22 22 23 24

" One of the "Brothers Swanson" by Jerry Lewis

I was driving down the street in my Datsun
the first time I heard [my own song on the
radio]. It wasn't that I couldn't believe it—
it's simply that my heart dropped to my
knees. (*Insider,* 1978)

RECORD FACTORY

99 Park Lane   •   Brisbane, California 94005   •   (415) HOT-4000

OAKLAND

It doesn't seem like me. . . .
When I hear "Soft and Wet"
on the radio, it seems like
someone else is singing.
(*Right On!,* 1979)

164

PART III.

CONTRO-
VERSY

I spent too much money in the studio for the first album, so they looked at me like, here's a child in here trying to do a man's job. Like I said, I'm really stubborn and I strive for the best, so I tried to do the best the second time around and make a hit and do it for the least amount of money. My second album cost $35,000, but the first one cost four times that amount. The second sold a lot more than the first. The third album [*Dirty Mind*, 1980] started out as demo tapes. I said to myself, "If I could put my bloodstream on vinyl, then this is what it would be." It was like that. (*Ebony*, 1986)

2 col. heads

PRINCE

PRINCE

PRINCE

1 col. heads

PRINCE PRINCE

PRINCE PRINCE

Prince. He scored big with the soul/disco hit "Soft And Wet" from his debut LP. His second, produced, arranged, composed and performed by Prince, includes the single "I Wanna Be Your Lover," "Why You Wanna Treat Me So Bad?" and "It's Gonna Be Lonely."

On Warner Bros. Records and Tapes
Mfr. list price $7.98 (Tapes $7.98)

On Warner Bros. Records and Tapes
On Warner Bros. Records and Tapes

On Warner Bros. Records and Tapes
On Warner Bros. Records and Tapes

1½" Cover / 9 Picas

65 Line Screen (Newspaper)

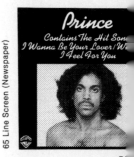

65 Line Screen (Newspaper)

65 Line Screen (Newspaper)

100 Line Screen

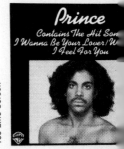

65 Line Screen (Newspaper)

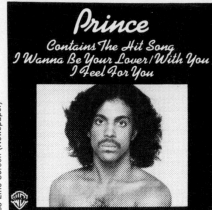

BSK 3366

BSK 3150

65 Line Screen (Newspaper)

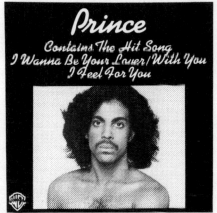

BSK 3366

55 Line Screen (Newspaper)

BSK 3150

65 Line Screen (Newspaper)

BSK 3150

100 Line Screen

BSK 3366

100 Line Screen

BSK 3150

More than my songs have to do with sex, they have to do with one human's love for another, which goes deeper than anything political that anybody could possibly write about. The need for love, the need for sexuality, basic freedom, equality . . . I'm afraid these things don't necessarily come out. I think my problem is that my attitude's so sexual that it overshadows anything else—that I might not mature enough as a writer to bring it all out yet.
(*Melody Maker,* 1981)

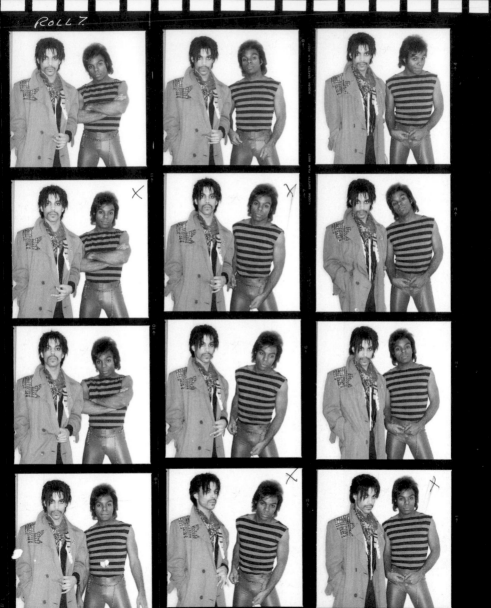

ROLL 7.

We were just fooling around, and we were jamming at the time. It was summertime, and we were having fun. And that's what I had on. But my coat was closed, so the photographer didn't know. I was with some friends and . . . I mean, if you've got a big coat on . . . I mean, who knows what he has on? I mean, it was hot out. Everybody was saying, "Why you got that hot coat on?" I'd say, "I'm really not that hot." And they'd say, "You gotta be." (*Musician,* 1983)

Dirty Mind

There's something about you, baby
It happens every time.
Whenever I'm around you baby
I get a dirty mind
It doesn't matter where we are
Doesn't matter who's around
It doesn't matter I just wanna lay you down

~~In quick~~ ~~bike you for a ride~~
in my daddy's car.
It's you, I really wanna drive
but you never go too far.

I ~~guess~~ ~~I'm~~ ~~the regular kinda~~ man
I may not be your style, but honey,
All I wanna do is just love you for a little while—
~~just a little while.~~

~~I really get a dirty mind~~
~~whenever you're around~~
if you got the time
I'll give you ~~some~~ money
to buy ~~a~~ dirty mind.
Don't ~~misunderstand~~ me
I ~~don't~~ fool around, but honey
you ~~never~~ got me on my knees, won't you please let me,
lay you down

After Bass Solo

I really get a dirty mind, whenever you're around
It happens to me every time,
You ~~just~~ just got a let me ~~gotta go~~ go lay ya, gotta let me
lay ya, lay ya, Repeat, down over
in my.

in my daddy's car
It's you I really wanna drive
Underneath the stars.
And I really got a dirty mind
whenever you're around
I don't wanna hurt you, baby
I only wanna lay you down

I wear what I wear because I don't like
clothes. This is what's most comfortable.
(*The Minneapolis Star*, 1980)

KODAK SAFETY FILM 5035   KODAK SAFETY FILM 5(

KODAK SAFETY FILM 5035   KODAK SAFETY FILM

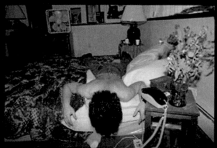

watch one of his gigs when I was about
5. We were supposed to stay in the car,
but I snuck out and went into the bar.
He was up on stage and it was amazing.
I remembered thinking, "These people
think my dad is great." I wanted to be
part of that. . . .

When I first played the *Dirty Mind* album
for him he said, "You're swearing on the
record. Why do you have to do that?" And
I said, "Because I swear." We got into this
whole big thing about what you can and
can't do on record. The point for me is that
you can do anything you want. My goal
is to excite and to provoke on every level.
(*Los Angeles Times*, 1982)

Do Me, Baby
Like you never done before.
SSSSSSlll Oooo Give it to me
Til I just can't take no more

Here we are in this big ol' empty room
Staring each other down, Baby I know
You want me just as much as I want you,
Let's stop fooling around
Your love is so good to me
You do it like nobody can
Take me baby Kiss me all over
Play with my love.
Bring out what's been in me, far too long
That's all I been dreaming of.

There's nothing like the feeling after you've
done something and play it back, and
you know that you'll never hear anything
like it and that they'll never figure it

VAGINA (HALF-BOY, HALF-GIRL)

HAD THE WORLDS BEST OF
SAW BOTH WORLDS

VAGINA WAS HALF-~~GIRL~~ BOY, HALF-~~BOY~~ GIRL
HER HAIR WAS SHORTER THAN MINE
SHE TOLD ME SHE LIVED IN THE CITY.
I NEVER KNEW WHEN SHE WAS LYING.
I 1st SAW HER IN A GAY BAR, KISSING ANOTHER GIRL
I TOLD HER, ~~BABY I'M A~~ "LOOKING FOR A TURN, AND SHE SAID...
"WELCOME TO MY WORLD" "WELCOME TO MY WORLD"
VAGINA WAS HALF-BOY, HALF-GIRL
SHE ~~TAUGHT~~ SHOWED ME HOW TO DANCE
WE USED TO DO IT, USED TO DO IT WITH THE T.V. ON,
IN A POLITICAL ROMANCE.
HALF-BOY! HALF-GIRL! THE BEST OF BOTH WORLDS!
" " " " " " " "

2. VAGINA WAS ~~HALF-BOY~~, ~~HALF-GIRL~~
SHE HAD HER OWN WAY OF DOING THINGS
MY BABY, SHE SHOULDA BEEN KING,
'CAUSE SHE WAS STRONG, BUT SO UNDERSTANDING.
BRIDGE

3. VAGINA, HALF-BOY, HALF-GIRL
~~YOU~~ NEVER TOLD ME HOW ~~YOU~~ GOT ~~YOUR~~ HER NAME
GUESS ~~YOU~~ SHE WANTED A LITTLE FAME.
I ~~GUESS~~ ~~YOU~~ GOT ~~WHAT~~ ~~YOU~~ WANTED.
WELL, I GUESS YOU GOT WHAT YOU WANTED HOW SHE
SHE NEVER TOLD ME
GOT HER NAME

A B C D E F G A
L M N O P
Q R S T U V W X Y Z

CHANT — HALF-BOY, HALF-GIRL
THE BEST OF BOTH WORLDS

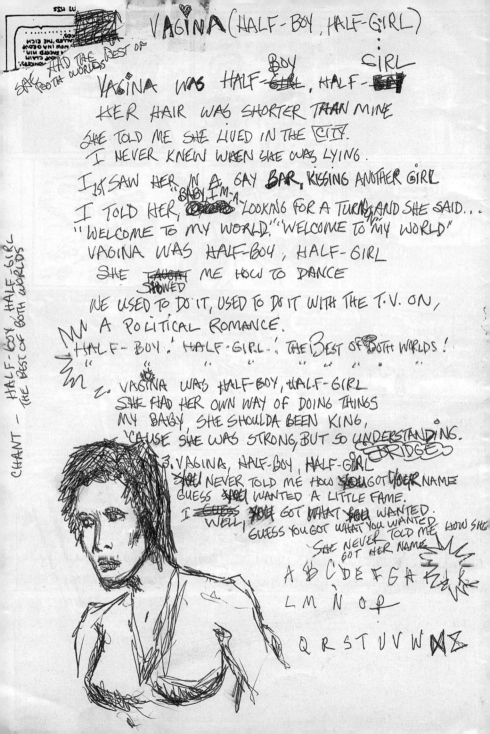

When I first got started in music, I was
attracted by the same things that attract
most people to this business. I wanted
to impress my friends and I wanted to
make money. For a while, I just did it as
a hobby. Then it turned into a job and
a way to eat. Now I look on it as art.
I realized after *Dirty Mind* that I can get
away with anything I want to get away
with. All I have to do is be true to myself.
I can make the records I want to make
and still be OK. I feel free. (*Los Angeles
Times,* 1982)

WE DON'T GIVE A DAMN, WE JUST WANNA JAM

COOL BAG, IS SUCH A DOUBLE DRAG, PARTY UP
GOTTA, GOTTA GOTTA PARTY UP (PARTY UP, GOT TO PARTY UP)

GOT TO PARTY DOWN BABY REVOLUTIONARY ROCK'N'ROLL
GOING UPTOWN BABY

~~HOW YOU GONNA MAKE ME KILL~~
~~JUST TAKE A CHANCE, COME ON AND DANCE~~

THEY GOT A DRIFT, I JUST LAUGH & P.U.
FIGHTING WAR, SUCH A FUCKIN' BORE, P.U.

GOT TO PARTY DOWN, BABY, IT'S ALL ABOUT - WHATS IN YOUR MIND
GOING UPTOWN, BABY, WANNA DIE, JUST WANNA HAVE A
                                        BLOODY GOOD TIME

BECAUSE OF THEIR HALF-BAKED MISTAKES
WE GET ICE CREAM, NO CAKE
ALL LIES, NO TRUTH, IS IT FAIR TO KILL
                            THE
                                YOUTH

I think I change constantly, because I can hear the music changing. The other day I put my first three albums on and listened to the difference. And I know why I don't sound like that anymore. Because things that made sense to me and things that I liked then, I don't like anymore. The way I played music, just the way I was in love a lot back then when I used to make those records. And love meant more to me then—but now I realize that people don't always tell you the truth, you know? I was really gullible back then. I believed in everybody around me. . . . If someone said something good to me, I believed it. . . . And I felt good when I was singing back then.

The things I do now, I feel anger sometimes when I sing, and I can hear the difference. I'm screaming more now than I used to. And things like that. I think it's just me. It also has to do with the instrumentation. It has nothing to do with trying to change styles or anything. Plus, I'm in a different environment; I see New York a little bit more. In my subconscious I'm influenced by the sinisterness of it, you know, the power. I hear sirens all the time, things like that. It's not like that in Minneapolis. If you ever go there you'll see it's real laid-back: real quiet, and you have to make your own action. I think a lot of warped people come out of there. My friends. I know a lot of warped girls, okay? Warped to me means they see things differently than I would, I suppose. They talk a lot. They talk a lot about nothing. But I mean heavy. They get into it like you wouldn't believe. I mean, we could get into an hour-long conversation about my pants. You know, why they're so tight, or something, do you know what I mean? (*Musician*, 1983)

1982, I wrote that. We were sitting around watching a special about 1999, and a lot of people were talking about the year and speculating on what was gonna happen. And I just found it real ironic how everyone that was around me—whom I thought to be very optimistic people—were dreading those days. And I always knew I'd be cool. I never felt like this was gonna be a rough time for me. I knew there were gonna be rough times for the earth, because this system is based in entropy and it's pretty much headed in a certain direction. So, I just wanted to write something that gave hope. And what I find is people listen to it, and no matter where we are in the world, I always get the same type of response from them. (*Larry King Live,* 1999)

1999

I was ~~trippin'~~ dreamin' when I wrote this ~~so~~ forgive me if it's ~~goes~~ astray.
~~But~~ When I woke up this morning coulda sworn it was ~~judgement~~ judgement day.
The sky ~~was~~ all purple, there were people running
~~~~ everywhere ~~~~ and you know I didn't
~~Trying to run~~ from destruction ~~~~ baby ~~~~ even
care... cuz

{ They say... 2000-party over, — oops, out of time.
{ So tonight I'm gonna party like it's 1999!

I was ~~trippin'~~ when I wrote this ~~so~~ sue me if I go
too fast
But life is just a party and parties ~~~~ were not meant to
last.
War's all around us, my mind says ~~prepare~~
to fight.
~~~~ if I gotta die I'm gonna listen to my body tonight.
(CHORUS) ~~Baby, let me tell you something...~~
~~~~ if you didn't come to party don't bother knockin'
on my door
I got a lion in my pocket and baby he's ready to roar.
Everybody's got a bomb we could all die any
Before I let·   day I'll
~~~~ -that happen... ~~I'm gonna~~ dance my life away.
(CHORUS)

PRINCE
1999
PRODUCED, ARRANGED, COMPOSED
AND PERFORMED* BY PRINCE

1. 1999 · 6:22
2. LITTLE RED CORVETTE · 4:58
3. DELIRIOUS · 3:56

All songs published by Controversy Music ASCAP
℗ 1982 Warner Bros. Records Inc. for the U.S. & WEA
International Inc. for the world outside of the U.S.
© 1982 Warner Bros. Records Inc. for the U.S. & WEA
International Inc. for the world outside of the U.S.
A Warner Communications Company

PRINCE
1999
PRODUCED, ARRANGED, COMPOSED
AND PERFORMED* BY PRINCE

1. LET'S PRETEND WE'RE MARRIED · 7:20
2. D.M.S.R. · 8:05

All songs published by Controversy Music ASCAP
℗ 1982 Warner Bros. Records Inc. for the U.S. & WEA
International Inc. for the world outside of the U.S.
© 1982 Warner Bros. Records Inc. for the U.S. & WEA
International Inc. for the world outside of the U.S.
A Warner Communications Company

BLK

Little Red Corvette

I guess I should known by the way you parked your
car sideways that it wouldn't last.
You see You're the kinda person that believes in making
out once... Love em' and leave 'em fast.
I guess I must be dumb, caz you had a pocketful of
horses,— Trojan and some of 'em used.
But it was Saturday night, I guess that makes it
alright. and you say what have I got to lose?

and I say Little Red Corvette   Baby you ~~~~ much too fast
Little Red Corvette   You need a love that's gonna last.
Little Red Corvette   Baby you got to slow down
'Cause if you don't, you' gonna run your Little Red
Corvette right in the ground.

I guess I shoulda closed my eyes when you drove
me to the place where your horses run free cause
I felt a little ill when I saw all the pictures of the
jockeys that were there before me.
Believe it or not ~~~~~~~~~~~~~ it, I started to worry—I wondered
If I had enough class.
But it was Saturday night, I guess that makes it
alright and a say, have Baby ~~ got enough gas?
~~ Chorus ~~ ~~ Chorus ~~ ~~ Chorus ~~

A body like yours ought to be in jail
cause it's on the verge of being obscene!
Move over, baby give me the keys I'm gonna
try to ~~wreck~~ tame your little red love machine. Tenacity!
Solo ~~ Chorus ~~

Ad lib: Girl you got an ass like, you know, I've never seen.
and the ride is so smooth you sure this ain't a limosine.
Cush, cush cushion in a velvet sweat,
Suck it all night so you don't forget! Mayday.

The most important thing is to be true to yourself, but I also like danger. That's what is missing from pop music today. There's no excitement and mystery—people sneaking out and going to these forbidden concerts by Elvis Presley or Jimi Hendrix. I'm not saying I'm better than anybody else, but I don't feel like there are a lot of people out there telling the truth in their music. (*Los Angeles Times*, 1982)

PART IV.

BABY I'M A STAR

This is the story of the dreams and aspirations of 3 ~~individuals~~.—Morris Day, a ~~~~ good-looking, cool 22-year old part-time musician, part-time pimp, part-time dreamer. Morris loves music, money and women. ~~The~~ These 3 vices usually conflict with each other and the end result is something he finds hard to deal with.—Being stuck in the ghetto.// The 2nd ~~individual~~ comes from a well-to-do family. She is very attractive and she knows it. Thus she named herself—Vanity. Her real name is ~~~~ Louise but she changed it because of her lifelong hang-up.—She wants to be "accepted (one of the gang." She thinks she doesn't fit in. In reality she doesn't. She's too rich, too pretty, and too much a prude. She ~~needs~~ friend, but she works too hard at it. She's ~~to~~ viewed as a phony "rich bitch" by most of the kids in every new neighborhood she's ever moved into. She's only 17 and still hangs on to high-school "games." Mind games. But ~~~~ underneath she's a very loving human being. It's just that no one's had the patience to tame her.

The 3rd individual is Prince—the main character. Named by his musician father Prince grew up alone. ~~Raised by relative~~ ~~in the neighborhood.~~ When he was young, 6 or 7 years old, he watched as his mother shot his father dead then turned the gun on herself. Crazed by jealousy she made Prince's father's life miserable by her incessant drinking, cursing and craving for sex. All she wanted was a good time.

Prince's father on the other hand was a wise but stubborn ~~God~~ fearing man who only wanted a ~~clean~~ quiet Christian home to ~~come~~ to. After spending the night in some sleazy ~~bar~~ nightclub he worked part time to keep food on the table. But what he usually got was a drunk wife who forgot to fix dinner, a crying baby boy and complaining neighbors fed up with the ~~loud~~ volume his wife ~~was~~ keeps playing the stereo.

Prince's father had one bad habit. When he'd come home to a situation like this he would go beserk and beat his wife.

Going beserk meant while quoting scriptures from the ~~Bible.~~ Good book he would proceed to bloody his wife's face.

He would always beg forgiveness later and forgive she would. Except the last time.

So much time is spent explaining Prince's parents because it explains why 3 doctors diagnosed Prince as a "mentally disturbed" young man with a "split" personality.

Prince is 19 years old and has spent one half of his life playing music and the other half trying to figure out who he really is. Is he his mother — drinking and swearing and coming on to another human like it's the only chance he'll get. Or is he his father conducting life as though God were watching every breath. Chauvinistic, stubborn and quick to explode. This poses a problem for Prince's friends who are also his fellow band members. One minute he's a sweet quiet little introvert. The next he's either screaming the book of Revelation to someone or he's drunk in the corner of some bar — masturbating.

This uncertainty in Prince's character has made for some interesting concerts for him and his band the Revolution.

Sometimes jolted by flashbacks in which he sees ~~through~~ visions of his past through ~~his~~, his mother, ~~his~~ his father ~~or~~, ~~his~~ or his own eyes, Prince "trips out" so to speak right in the middle of songs sometimes throwing his band for a loop.

They're not sure if he's really a ~~psycho or~~ psycho or if it's all an act. As is the audience.

But Prince wants to make it. Bad. He wants fame and fortune and everything that goes ~~with all the~~ with it. Sure. But most of all he wants to help people through his music. Whether it's a cure for loneliness, a beat to make them dance or a message so that they can better understand themselves. He most of all wants to feel he's done something worthwhile in his life. Scoring points with God I guess. That's his father talking.

This movie deals with a period in which all of these characters must face the realities of life. "If there's something out there that u want - Go for it! Nothing comes to sleepers but dreams."

The city Morris, Vanity and Prince live in is appropriately divided into three sections. Morris lives downtown. The ghetto. Predominately Black and Poverty-stricken. People who live here don't have much so they go out of their way to look as though they do. People ~~too~~ downtown take pride in their appearance especially when they're out for a night on the town.

Zoot suits, wide-brimmed hats and Stacey Adams shoes are common. Morris and his band the Time are known for their "cool" attire. Morris has several women who "work" for him. No one knows for sure what kind of "work" the women do, but they have a pretty good idea.

Vanity lives in the suburbs. The rich part of town. "Green Acres." as termed by the people "downtown." Beautiful farmland and lakes accent the area. Most of the parents who live here are very snobbish and strict. The downtown area night clubs are off limits to ~~the~~ most teenagers. By their parents orders of course.

Most of the kids downtown dislike ~~don't~~
the preppy-looking rich kids from
"Green Acres" and occasional fights break
out. So parents figure their kids should
hang out in their own clique. Vanity's
parents especially.

Prince lives "Uptown." Middle
class and very ~~big~~ ~~Puerto~~ liberal. ~~neighbor and~~
People from all walks of life live
in Uptown. White, Black, Puerto Rican
Gay, Straight. Young and old. Life here
is very laid-back. Many artists of various
types come here ~~to work~~ because of the
peaceful atmosphere. Prince being born
of Italian and Black decent ~~was born~~
in the downtown area and was moved
Uptown by relatives when his parents
passed away. Prince and ~~the~~ Revolution
are the hottest band uptown mainly because
of their avant-garde approach to pop. They have
developed a sort of beatnik following in
their short time they play all original
music and have a reputation for their
bizarre way of dressing.

When Prince was young he watched his ~~parents~~ mother shoot his father dead and then turn the gun on herself. Thus he has flashbacks throughout the flick which cause him to act either like his mother or his father. (One interesting aspect of the film is that during the dream sequences in which Prince envisions his parents, they are portrayed by Prince himself.) ~~Prince's~~ His band members are ~~an~~ interesting lot. There are 5 of them including one girl—Lisa who is very ~~attr~~ alluring and Matt Fink who dropped out of pre-med school to play rock 'n' roll but forgot to drop ~~it~~ off the surgeon's outfit. He is very funny.

~~Morris' band members are acces~~

There is a confrontation between Prince and the Time when the time travel Uptown to one of Prince's gigs to check out their "competition. This is the 1st time Prince and Morris lay eyes on Vanity who is there out of curiousity and is genuinely impressed by Prince.

She of course wants to play both sides of the fence which she tries to do throughout most of the film. Vanity really digs Prince but she is amused by Morris who constantly has an entourage to help him with every day tasks like combing his hair and removing his overcoat.

The film then focuses on Prince's psychological difficulties and how his band members cope with them. A few more gigs are shown with Prince "tripping out" reverting into either his mother or his father. All the while deeply interested in seeing Vanity again.

She turns up strangely enough at one the Time's gigs invited there by Morris. She is intoxicated. Vanity is much like Prince's mother in his eyes anyway. (When Prince portrays his mother he wears hoop earrings that were she mother's favorite. Vanity wears some that are similar. This alone causes him to flashback.) Prince and Morris don't exactly hit it off. For reasons that are understandable.

They make various comments to one another about each others lifestyle which is a basic threat to the film. They try to make friends with Vanity & help to no avail.

Several comic subplots involving the Time (Morris' troubles with his girls, a house party that gets an uninvited guest — a bat.), Prince and Morris trying to kidnap Vanity at the same time when she gets grounded for going downtown to watch the Time. Prince climbs in Vanity's window, Morris climbs in Vanity's mom's window. Her husband away on a business trip. Prince gets the prize this time and there is a torrid fight-love scene between him & Vanity when Prince during one of his flashbacks believes Vanity is his mother and he is his father.

The movie climaxes with a battle of the bands between Prince and the Time with the time being victorious because of Prince's erratic stage presence. Switching between his mother and his father he throws the band completely off by quoting the bible in between cursing the audience for being sinners all the while crying and singing the torments of being a schizophrenic.

Vanity rushes to his side. He loses the battle but gets the girl. Deserted by his band fed up with his unpredictable persona, Prince leaves the club totally bewildered. Vanity stays the night with him. The two lie on the bed and drift off to sleep. (Camera pans away. Camera comes back to them lying in a different position to give impression of hours passing. Prince rises from the bed, goes to dresser and pulls out the same pistol his mother used to shoot his father and then kill herself.

He raises it to his head. There is shot. Camera cuts to Prince rising from the bed screaming - realizing it was all a dream. Credits roll.

Songs include

Baby I'm A STAR
 I WOULD DIE FOR U
MOONBEAM LEVELS
 I CAN'T STOP THIS FEELING I GOT
 TOO TOUGH
WOULDN'T U LOVE TO LOVE ME
 I JUST WANNA BE RICH
  BOLD GENERATION
            Among others.

THIS IS THE STORY OF

the dreams and aspirations of 3 individuals. 1.—Morris Day—, a good-looking, cool 22-year-old part-time musician, part-time pimp, part-time dreamer. Morris loves music, money, and women. These 3 vices usually conflict with each other and the end result is something he finds hard to deal with—Being stuck in the ghetto.

The 2nd individual comes from a well-to-do family. She is very attractive and she knows it. Thus she named herself—Vanity. Her real name is Louise but she changed it because of her lifelong hang-up—she wants to be "accepted" (one of the gang). She thinks she doesn't fit in. In reality she doesn't. She's too rich, too pretty, and too much a prude. She needs friends, but she works too hard at it. She's viewed as a phony "rich bitch" by most of the kids in every new neighborhood she's ever moved into. She's only 17 and still hangs on to high school "games." Mind games. But underneath she's a very loving human being. It's just that no one's had the patience to tame her.

The 3rd individual is Prince—the main character. Named by his musician father, Prince grew up alone. When he was young, 6 or 7 years old, he watched as his mother shot his father dead then turned the gun on herself. Crazed by jealousy she made Prince's father's life miserable by her incessant drinking, cursing, and craving for sex. All she wanted was a good time.

Prince's father, on the other hand, was a wise but stubborn God-fearing man who only wanted a clean, quiet, Christian home to come to after spending the night in some sleazy nightclub he worked [at] part-time to keep food on the table. But what he usually got was a drunk wife who forgot to fix dinner, a crying baby boy, and complaining neighbors fed up with the volume his wife keeps playing the stereo.

Prince's father had one bad habit. When he'd come home to a situation like this he would go berserk and beat his wife. Going berserk meant while quoting scripture from the Good Book he would proceed to bloody his wife's face.

He would always beg forgiveness later and forgive she would. Except the last time.

So much time is spent explaining Prince's parents because it explains why 3 doctors diagnosed Prince as a "mentally disturbed" young man with a "split personality." Prince is 19 years old and has spent one half of his life playing music and the other half trying to figure out who he really is. Is he his mother—drinking and swearing and coming on to another human like it's the only chance he'll get? Or is he his father, conducting life as though God were watching every breath—chauvinistic, stubborn, and quick to explode? This poses a problem for Prince's friends who are also his fellow band members. One minute he's a sweet, quiet little introvert. The next he's either screaming the book of Revelation to someone or he's drunk in the corner of some bar—masturbating.

This uncertainty in Prince's character has made for some interesting concerts for him and his band the Revolution. Sometimes jolted by flashbacks in which he sees visions of his past through his mother, his father, or his own eyes, Prince "trips out" so to speak right in the middle of songs sometimes, throwing his band for a loop. They're not sure if he's really a psycho or if it's all an act. [Neither] is the audience.

But Prince wants to make it. Bad. He wants fame and fortune and everything that goes with it. Sure. But most of all he wants to help people through his music. Whether it's a cure for loneliness, a beat to make them dance, or a message so that they can better understand themselves, he most of all wants to feel he's done something worthwhile in his life. Scoring points with God, I guess.

That's his father talking.

This movie deals with a period in which all 3 of the characters must face the realities of life. "If there's something out there that u want—Go for it! Nothing comes to sleepers but dreams."

The city Morris, Vanity, and Prince live in is appropriately divided into three sections. Morris lives downtown. The ghetto.

Predominantly black and poverty-stricken. People who live here don't have much so they go out of their way to look as though they do. People downtown take pride in their appearance, especially when they're out for a night on the town. Zoot suits, wide-brimmed hats, and Stacy Adams shoes are common. Morris and his band the Time are known for their "cool" attire. Morris has several women who "work" for him. No one knows for sure what kind of "work" the women do, but they have a pretty good idea.

Vanity lives in the suburbs. The rich part of town. "Green Acres," as termed by the people "downtown." Beautiful farmland and lakes accent the area. Most of the parents who live here are very snobbish and strict. The downtown area nightclubs are off-limits to most teenagers. By their parents' orders of course. Most of the kids downtown dislike the preppy-looking rich kids from Green Acres and occasional fights break out. So parents figure their kids should hang out in their own clique. Vanity's parents especially.

Prince lives "Uptown." Middle-class and very liberal. People from all walks of life live in Uptown. White, Black, Puerto Rican. Gay. Straight. Young and old. Life here is very laid-back. Many artists of various types come here to work because of the peaceful atmosphere. Prince, being born of Italian and Black descent was born in the downtown area and was moved Uptown by relatives when his parents passed away. Prince and the Revolution are the hottest band uptown, mainly because of their avant-garde approach to pop. They have developed a sort of beatnik following in their short time together. They play all original music and have a reputation for their bizarre way of dressing.

When Prince was young he watched his mother shoot his father dead and then turn the gun on herself. Thus he has flashbacks throughout the flick which cause him to act either like his mother or his father. (One interesting aspect of the film is that during the dream sequences in which Prince envisions his parents, they are portrayed by Prince himself.) His band members are an interesting lot. There are 5 of them including one girl, Lisa, who is very alluring, and Matt Fink, who dropped out of premed school to play rock 'n' roll but forgot to drop off the surgeon's outfit. He is very funny.

There is a confrontation between Prince and the Time when the Time travel Uptown to one of Prince's gigs to check out their "competition." This is the 1st time Prince and Morris lay eyes on Vanity, who is there out of curiosity and is genuinely impressed by Prince.

She of course wants to play both sides of the fence, which she tries to do throughout most of the film. Vanity really digs Prince, but she is amused by Morris who constantly has an entourage to help him with everyday tasks like combing his hair and removing his overcoat.

The film then focuses on Prince's psychological difficulties and how his band members cope with them. A few more gigs are shown with Prince "tripping out" turning into either his mother or his father. All the while deeply interested in seeing Vanity again.

She turns up, strangely enough, at one [of] the Time's gigs, invited there by Morris. She is intoxicated. Vanity is much like Prince's mother, in his eyes, anyway. (When Prince portrays his mother, he wears hoop earrings that were his mother's favorite. Vanity wears some that are similar. This alone causes him to flash back.) Prince and Morris don't exactly hit it off. For reasons that are understandable.

They make various comments to one another about each other's lifestyle, which is a basic thread to the film. They try to make friends with Vanity's help, to no avail.

Several comic subplots involving the Time (Morris's troubles with his girls, a house party that gets an uninvited guest—a bat) Prince and Morris trying to kidnap Vanity at the same time when she gets grounded for going downtown to watch the Time. Prince climbs in Vanity's window, Morris climbs in Vanity's mom's window. Her husband's away on a business trip. Prince gets the prize this time and there is a torrid fight-love scene between him & Vanity when Prince, during one of his flashbacks, believes Vanity is his mother and he is his father.

The movie climaxes with a battle of the bands between Prince and the Time, with the Time being victorious because of Prince's erratic stage presence. Switching between his mother and his father, he throws the band completely off by quoting the bible in between cursing the audience for being sinners, all the while crying and singing the torments of being a schizophrenic.

Vanity rushes to his side. He loses the battle but gets the girl. Deserted by his band, fed up with his unpredictable persona, Prince leaves the club totally bewildered. Vanity stays the night with him. The two lie on the bed and drift off to sleep. (Camera pans away. Camera comes back to them lying in a different position to give impression of hours passing.) Prince rises from the bed, goes to [the] dresser and pulls out the same pistol his mother used to shoot his father then kill herself.

He raises it to his head. There is [a] shot. Camera cuts to Prince rising from the bed screaming—realizing it was all a dream. Credits roll.

Dearly Beloved we are gathered here
today to get through this thing called
life.
Electric word- Life. It means forever!
and that's an awful long time.
But I'm here to tell u that there's
something else. The After World.
That's right.
A world of never-ending happiness.
You can always see the sun - day
or night.
So when u call up that shrink in
Beverly Hills, you know the one,
Dr. Everything'll Be Alright, instead
of asking him how much of your mind
is left, ask him - how much of your time.
'Cause in this life things are much harder
than in the After World. In this life
you're on your own.
So u better try to be happy 'cause
one day the sun may set for good.
If De elevator tries to bring u
down play crazy and punch a higher floor.

My original draft of "Let's Go Crazy" was
much different from the version that wound
up being released. As I wrote it, "Let's Go
Crazy" was about God and the deelevation
of sin. But the problem was that religion
as a subject is taboo in pop music. People
think that the records they release have
got to be hip, but what I need to do is to
tell the truth. (*Musician*, 1997)

Let's Go Crazy

If u don't like the world You're livin in
Take a look around'a   at least u got friends
I called my old lady for a friendly word.
She picked up the phone and dropped it on the
              floor. Ah-sss, Ah-sss was all I heard.
But Um gonna let de elevator bring me down.
NO NO LET'S GO

Chorus!   Let's Go Crazy   Let's Go nuts
Look the purple Banana   til they put (you)(me)
              in the truck, let's Go nuts.
We're all excited but we don't know why
         Maybe it's because we're all gonna die
And when we do. What's it all for?
We better live now before the Grim Reaper
    comes knockin' on our door. Get Upa
    Are we gonna let de elevator bring us down.
NO NO LET'S GO! CHORUS
We Won't let de elevator bring us
"   "   "   "   "   " "
"   "   "   "   "   " " down, down, down.
         Let's Go!
Dr. Everything'll be alright will make
         everything go wrong.
Pills and thrills and dafodils will kill.
    Hang tough it won't be long He's comin.

I had to change those words up, but
the elevator was Satan. I had to change
the words up because you couldn't say
God on the radio. And "Let's Go Crazy"
was God to me. It was: Stay happy, stay
focused, and you can beat the elevator.
(*VH1 to One,* 1997)

Computer Blue

Where or where is my lovelife where or where
can it be?

~~Doddy~~ ~~Nobody~~ ~~comes to see~~

Is there must be something wrong with the machinery?

All fall down with icky cellophane love affairs.
Computer blue.

Why does my girl sleep with other boys. Can u tell
computer why? Well I guess...

Until. I find that righteous one.
Forever Computer Blue.

Where or where is my patience. Where or where
has it gone.

If you really love me why'd you go away computer
never wrong.

You say you want relationship based on give and take.
Tell u what: I'll give you a baby if u take a bath.

Until I find that righteous one.
Forever Computer Blue.

MIDDLE BRIDGE

over →

Where or where is my love life where or where
can it be.
there must be something wrong with ~~computer~~ the machinery
all fall down with Elementary one night stands
Why can't you just be my woman and let me be
your man?

Until I find that righteous one
Forever computer blue.

2. I got a girl named Nikki
   I thank God that she's fine
   Twice she cooked me dinner
   Taste like shit both times
   Thank God Nikki's fine
   The girl can't cook but lawd she sure can grind.

1. I knew a girl named Nikki
   Guess you could say she's a sex fiend
   Met her in a hotel lobby
   Masturbating with a magazine.
   She said, how'd you like to waste some time
   and I couldn't resist when I saw little Nikki
               grind.

2. She took me to her castle
   Couldn't believe my eyes
   She had so many devices
   Everything money could buy
   She said, sign your name on the dotted line. The
   lights went out and Nikki started to grind.

4. I woke up the next morning
   Nikki wasn't there.
   I looked all over all I found was phone no. on the stairs.
   She said thank u for a funky time. Call me up whenever you want to grind.

3. The castle started spinning
   Or maybe it was my brain.
   I can't tell you what she did to me
   but my body will never be the same.
   Her lovin' 'll kick your behind.
   She won't show u no mercy but she'll
   sho'nuff show u, she'nuff how to grind.

Believe me, baby I know the
   times are changing.
It's time we all reach out
   4 something new.

You say you want a leader but
of you can't make up your
         mind. Then... I lot
Close your ~~eyes~~ and ~~follow~~
and your darling Prince ~~will~~
guide ~~please~~ u.

I don't want money I don't
         want love.
If I wanted either one, I would
         buy it.
I want the heavy stuff. What
your dreams are made of.
I want control. I've got the
keys now gimme ~~the~~ driver's
         seat. Try it.

I.

I never meant to fill
   your life with sorrow
I never meant to cause u
   any pain
I only wanted to one time see u
   laughing
"I only wanted to see u bathing
in the Purple Rain,
      Purple Rain
I only wanted to see u underneath
   the purple rain
         Repeat Chorus

1. I never wanted to be your weekend
         lover   some kind of
I only wanted to be your purple
         friend
Baby I could never steal u from another
It's such a shame our friendship had to
   end...

Before *Purple Rain,* all the kids who came
to First Avenue knew us, and it was just
like a big, fun fashion show. The kids would
dress for themselves and just try to look
really cool. Once you got your thing right,
you'd stop looking at someone else. You'd
be yourself, and you'd feel comfortable.
(*Rolling Stone,* 1985)

228

I promise I won't hurt u.
Trust Me,
Trust Me,
~~Trust Me~~,
I'm not a politician, I'm
a purple musician.
and I only want to set u
free.

Trust Me
I only want to see u bathe
in the Purple Rain

I think *Purple Rain* is the most avant-
garde purple thing I've ever done. Just
look at "When Doves Cry" and "Let's
Go Crazy." Most black artists won't try
a groove like that. If more would, we'd
have more colorful radio stations. In
the sixties, when everybody tried to be
different, you had War and Santana,
and Hendrix, and Sly, and James, and
they were all uniquely different. Now,
everyone just jumps on what they think
are the hottest sounds. . . . Sometimes
I just wish that when I turn on the radio
I could get that many different colors.
It's fun to hear a song like "Raspberry
Beret" on R&B. I'm not saying that I'm
great or anything like that; I'm just saying
that I'm an alternative. I'm something
else. And I long to hear something else
from everybody. (*Ebony,* 1986)

RASBERRY BERET

I WAS WORKING PART-TIME IN A
            FIVE & DIME, MY BOSS WAS MR. MᶜGEE
HE TOLD ME SEVERAL TIMES THAT HE DIDN'T
LIKE MY KIND, CAUSE I WAS A BIT TOO LEISURELY
EVERY OTHER DAY WAS THE SAME AS YESTERDAY
BUT A LITTLE BIT DIFFERENT THAN THE DAY BEFORE.
I WAS BUSY WASTING TIME WHEN THE STORE
 BELL CHIMED SHE CAME IN THROUGH THE OUT
 ~~STORE~~ DOOR.

chorus. SHE WORE A RASBERRY BERET
THE KIND YOU'D BUY IN A SECOND HAND STORE
RASBERRY BERET IF IT WAS WARM SHE WOULDN'T
WEAR MUCH MORE / RASBERRY BERET, I THINK I LOVE YOU.
WE DIDN'T STOP TALKING 'TIL WE CLOSED OUR EYES.
EXHAUSTED FROM THE LOVE WE MADE
ONLY CLEOPATRA COULD'VE EQUALED HER GRACE
 RUBY LIPS AND EYES OF JADE.
SHE TOLD ME OF HER TRAVELS, THE PLACES SHE'D GONE
AND THE MEN SHE HAD LOVED IN HER DAY.
SHE BEGGED ME TO TAKE HER AGAIN AND AGAIN
TO A PLACE ONLY A WOMAN CAN SAY. (CHORUS)
I WAS AWAKENED THAT MORNING BY THE SOUND
OF THE DOOR... MY GREEN EYES TURNED TO BLUE THERE WAS
A NOTE ON THE FLOOR. IT SAID, "THIS IS FOR YOU"
HER RASBERRY BERET IS ALL THAT I HAVE
OF MY LOVER TODAY. SHE WORE A...
            (CHORUS)

I'd like to take a moment and show love and appreciation for Lisa and Wendy.

I met Lisa first, she was in the band for a while, and then she introduced me to Wendy. When I first met Lisa, she didn't look me in the eye, I think—you'll have to ask her why. I called my manager and I said, "I don't think this is gonna work out. Can you make a plane reservation for her, she's going to have to go home." And then I said, "Hold on." And I could hear the piano coming from the basement. And she was playing something free-form—just making up these crazy chords that I never heard until I met Miles Davis, who came to my house and played similar chords. And she told me that her favorite piano player was Bill Evans. Right? I'm trying to imitate her now.

And I would write music and I would let them go to the studio and just mess around and see what they come up with. And Lisa wrote this harpsichord part that went: [plays opening bars of "Raspberry Beret"]. And that's the whole song, right? (First Piano & A Microphone performance, January 2016)

A lot of people have the idea that I'm a wild sexual person. It can be two o'clock in the afternoon, and someone will make a really strange request from the call box outside. One girl just kept pressing the buzzer. She kept pressing it, and then she started crying. I had no idea why. I thought she might have fallen down. I started talking to her, and she just kept saying, "I can't believe it's you." I said, "Big deal. I'm no special person. I'm no different than anyone." She said, "Will you come out?" I said, "Nope, I don't have much on." And she said, "That's okay."

I've lectured quite a few people out there. I'll say, "Think about what you're saying. How would you react if you were me?" I ask that question a lot. "How would you react if you were me?" They say, "Okay, okay." (*Rolling Stone*, 1985)

Your Kiss

U don't have 2 be beautiful, 2 turn me on
I just need your body baby from dusk til dawn
U don't need experience 2 turn me out
U just leave it all up 2 me I'll show u what it's all about

U don't have 2 be rich 2 be my girl
U "   "   "   "   " cool 2 rule my world
ain't no paticular sign I'm more compatible
I just want your extra time and your ★ ★ ★ ★ ★
KISS

U got 2 not talk dirty if u want 2 impress me
U can't be 2 flirty, I know how 2 undress me.
I wanna be your fantasy Maybe u could be mine
U just leave it all up 2 me We could have a good time!

CHORUS

Women not girls rule my world rule my world
Act your age not your shoe size maybe we can do the
twirl. Hit me.
U don't have 2 watch Dynasty 2 have an attitude
U just leave it all up 2 me, My love will be your
food.

CHORUS

I don't live in a prison. I am not afraid of anything. I haven't built any walls around myself, and I am just like anyone else. I need love and water, and I'm not afraid of a backlash because, like I say, there are people who will support my habits as I have supported theirs. I don't really consider myself a superstar. I live in a small town, and I always will. I can walk around and be me. That's all I want to be, that's all I ever tried to be. (MTV, 1985)

The Secretary of State
of the United States of America
hereby requests all whom it may concern to permit the citizen/
national of the United States named herein to pass
without delay or hindrance and in case of need to
give all lawful aid and protection.

Le Secrétaire d'Etat
des Etats-Unis d'Amérique
prie par les présentes toutes autorités compétentes de laisser passer
le citoyen ou ressortissant des Etats-Unis titulaire du présent passeport,
sans délai ni difficulté et, en cas de besoin de lui accorder
toute aide et protection légitimes.

CANCELLED
APR 25 1996

SIGNATURE OF BEARER/SIGNATURE DU TITULAIRE

UNITED STATES OF AMERICA

PASSPORT **PASSEPORT**	Type/Caté-gorie **P** — Code of issuing / code du pays State / Etat **USA** émetteur — PASSPORT NO./NO. DU PASSPORT **070610058**

Surname / Nom
NELSON
Given names / Prénoms
PRINCE ROGERS
Nationality / Nationalité
UNITED STATES OF AMERICA
Date of birth / Date de naissance
07 JUN/JUN 58
Sex / Sexe **M**   Place of birth / Lieu de naissance **MINNESOTA, U.S.A.**
Date of issue / Date de délivrance **05 JUN/JUN 86**   Date of expiration / Date d'expiration **04 JUN/JUN 96**
Authority / Autorité
PASSPORT AGENCY
SEATTLE
Amendments/ Modifications SEE PAGE **48**

```
P<USANELSON<<PRINCE<ROGERS<<<<<<<<<<<<<<<<<<
070610058USA5806078M9606047<<<<<<<<<<<<<<2
```

238

One day I might write the book about the hardships artists face. It's incredible that you write songs but don't own the rights to them, and someone else can do whatever they like with them. Still, my soul is cast iron and not to be dented. I've been on the mountaintop and seen what there is to see. I've been number one and sold huge amounts of records. My main concern is that I can now enjoy being a musician again. (*Top of the Pops,* 1997)

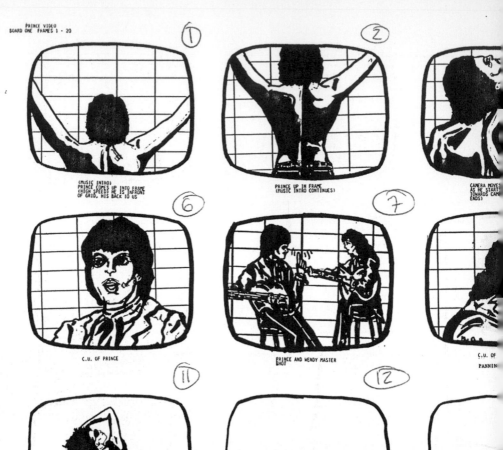

(1) (MUSIC INTRO) PRINCE COMES UP INTO FRAME (HIGH SPEED) HE IS IN FRONT OF GRID, HIS BACK TO US

(2) PRINCE UP IN FRAME (MUSIC INTRO CONTINUES)

CAMERA MOVES AS HE START TOWARDS CAM ENDS)

(6) C.U. OF PRINCE

(7) PRINCE AND WENDY MASTER SHOT

C.U. OF PANNIN

(11) LIGHTS COME UP TO REVEAL DANCER ON PLEXI SLAB (BACK TO US) SHE SPINS AND STARTS TO LIE DOWN

(12) DANCER LYING DOWN ON PLEXI SLAB

C.U. OF START O

(16) C.U. OF DANCER'S FACE WIPING FRAME

(17) MED. SHOT OF PRINCE

DANC SHA SHE PLU

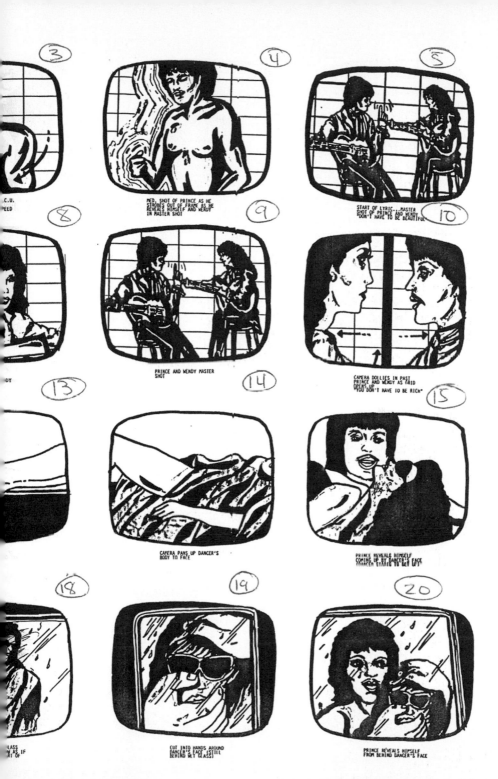

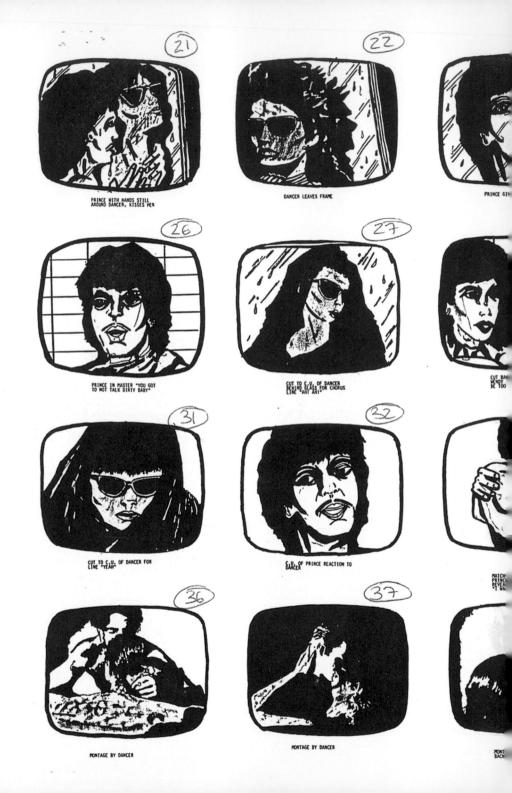

23

24
PRINCE LOOKS DOWN FOR
"HUH HUH.." LINE

25
CUT TO CLOSE UP OF PRINCE'S
GUITAR (BACK IN MASTER ROOM)

28

29
PRINCE IN MASTER ROOM
STARTS TO UNDO BELT
(GUITAR BEHIND HIS BACK)
"I KNOW HOW"

30
MATCH CUT TO PRINCE IN
FANTASY ROOM UNDOING PANTS
"TO UNDRESS ME"

33

34
MATCH CUT (IN SIZE) TO
PRINCE HOLDING DANCER BY
CHEST

35
MONTAGE BY DANCER

38

39
MED C.U. OF PRINCE TOUCHING
HIMSELF

40
CUT TO PRINCE SLIDING
TOWARDS DANCER'S
BREASTS

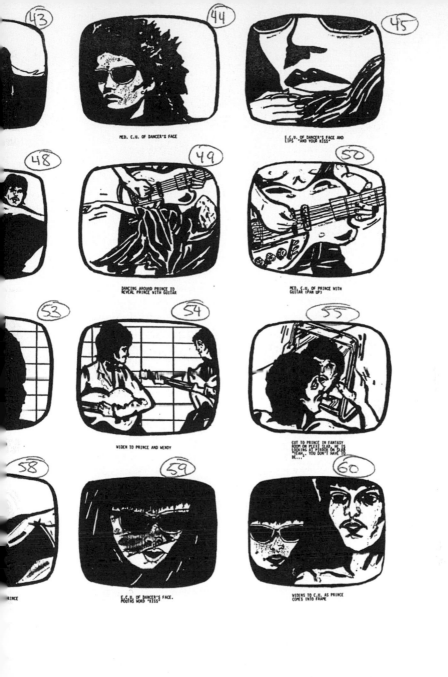

I can be upstairs at the piano, and Rande [my cook] can come in. Her footsteps will be in a different time, and it's real weird when you hear something that's a totally different rhythm than what you're playing. A lot of times that's mistaken for conceit or not having a heart. But it's not. And my dad's the same way, and that's why it was hard for him to live with anybody. I didn't realize that until recently. When he was working or thinking, he had a private pulse going constantly inside him. I don't know, your bloodstream beats differently. (*Rolling Stone*, 1985)

[My father] preaches all the time: "Strive to be different. It's OK to be different." . . . We have the same hands. We have the same dreams. We write the same lyrics, some-times. Accidentally, though. I'll write something and then I'll look up and he'll have the same thing already written. . . . The lyrics we write are similar, the same thing. With the music, we are a lot different. Our personalities are a lot alike, but his music is like nothing I've ever heard before. It's more complex. A lot of beautiful melodies are hidden beneath the complexity. That's why it takes me to pull all that out. That's why we work so well together. (*Ebony*, 1986)

If you dream something and go back to sleep, you forget it. But if you wake right up and stay up with it, you'll remember it and maybe get something out of it. I did that last night. I dreamt that my dad wrote a song and it was really a nice song. I remember that I woke up and really liked it, but I couldn't stay awake. (*The Minneapolis Star,* 1979)

Baby Baby, Baby what's it gonna be
" " " To it him or is it m
• Don't make me waste my time
• Don't make me lose my mind, baby

Baby, Baby Baby Can't u stay with me
" " " " Don't my kisses feel alrigh
• And u were so hard to find. The beautiful ones hurt u e
Paint a perfect picture. bring to life a v
She beautiful ones will always smash that picture. Always
$$ ——➤ • C Min Bridge

• If I told u baby that I'm in love with u
• " " " " " that I want go got married
                                              we
• You make me so confused. • The beautiful o

Baby, Baby Baby what's it gonna be C#
Baby, Baby Baby Do you want him? or do u

Cuz I want u said I want u
Baby, Baby, Baby The beautiful ones
                    But lemme tell ya
                    Sometime, Sometime
                    But Right now, Right n
                    I may not know where
                    I may not know what
                    But One thing for certain, bab
                    And to please u baby to please u
                                              cuz

tonight
they hunt u every time
~~every~~
~ in one's mind
rytime.

ld u think it was cool.
you always seem to lose.

r me

tives u lose
metime, sometime u win
so confused.
I want you,
my baby
eed
now what I want
I beg u down on my knees
Want u.. I Want y. baby

When I'm onstage, I'm out of body. That's
what the rehearsals, the practicing, the
playing is for. You work to a place where
you're all out of body. And that's when
something happens. You reach a plane of
creativity and inspiration. A plane where
every song that has ever existed and every
song that will exist in the future is right
there in front of you. And you just go with
it for as long as it takes. (*Essence*, 2014)

NOTES AND GUIDE TO PHOTOS

All images © The Prince Estate, except where noted.

P. II (frontispiece)
According to Prince's manager, Owen Husney, Prince came up with the concept for *For You*'s most famous photograph, which appears on the record's dust sleeve. Prince sits nude on a bed with an acoustic guitar, flanked by superimposed images of himself. The photo was taken by Joe Giannetti, a Minneapolis photographer, on a display bed at a Macy's in San Francisco. Before the Macy's shoot, Giannetti tried this more preliminary version on Husney's bed in Minneapolis. (Photos © 1986 Joseph Giannetti)

Introduction

P. 6 "The space in between the notes—that's the good part"
This wasn't the first time Prince had mused about the mechanics of funk. In a notebook from the late seventies, he dedicated some doggerel to the subject: "Words to fun by: 'To tap or not to tap / That is the question / Whether 'tis funkier on the three / than the one is to suffer the / slings and arrows of unsyncopated misfortune.' Willyum Shakespere."

P. 7 something that he described as "transcendence"
Prince was "in the zone" when he spent long hours at the piano; it felt "like an out-of-body experience," something akin to watching himself from the audience. See Alexis Petridis, "Prince: 'Transcendence. That's What You Want. When That Happens—Oh, Boy,'" *The Guardian,* November 12, 2015.

P. 10 "When it comes to your life story, don't let anyone else hold the pen."
"That would make a good song lyric," Prince said after paraphrasing Ramadan. See Jon Bream, "A Night with Prince: 'This Is Real Time,'" Minneapolis *Star Tribune,* May 19, 2013.

P. 35 "Have you ever just tried writing a hit?"
Stefani sang on Prince's "So Far, So Pleased" in 1999; he cowrote and coproduced No Doubt's song "Waiting Room." See Candice Rainey, "The All-Star: Gwen Stefani," *Elle,* May 4, 2011.

Part I.
The Beautiful Ones

P. 48
Prince's mother, Mattie Della Shaw, stands by a car in a photo dated December 25, 1956.

P. 50–77
Prince wrote these twenty-eight pages in early 2016, amid the same burst of retrospection that led to the Piano & A Microphone tour.

P. 78, TOP
Mattie Shaw stands by Prince at his crib in October 1958, when he was four months old. He was born on June 7, 1958. At the time, his parents lived in Minneapolis at 2201 5th Avenue S, apartment 203. He kept this photo in his vault.

P. 78, BOTTOM
Prince's father, John Nelson, sits at the piano in his Minneapolis home, March 1973.

P. 79–118
The spelling, style, and punctuation of Prince's handwritten pages have been preserved here. In rare cases, corrections have been made for clarity and missing words added in brackets. Chapter numbers have been added where they weren't present. Unless otherwise noted, all annotations come from Dan Piepenbring's February 2016 conversations with Prince.

P. 80
The Nelsons in a family photo from September 1964, taken outside of their home at 915 Logan Ave. N, Minneapolis. Mattie Della Shaw, top left; John Nelson, top right; Prince, bottom left, age six; his sister Tyka, bottom right, age four.

P. 81
Mattie sits by a record player in the Nelsons' living room, October 1958. Prince kept this photo in the vault.

P. 83
Prince playacts with a spear and helmet in the early sixties.

P. 87–89

Mattie wrote love notes to John, sometimes slipping them into the lunches she fixed him before he left for work. In one note from the late fifties, she writes, "You know it's a strange thing, the things I dream of, that is, you and me, in the house of our dream[s]. I keep picturing us in it, you in your smoking jacket, me in my lounging outfit, which I've already designed in my mind. Perhaps that's why I want you to buy us a hi-fi, because there's so many memories, so many words in records, in thoughts that you can put across that words can't reveal[.] It's almost an obsession in my mind. Our love I want to be a dream made into reality.

"If only you could see so deep down inside of me. When we have each other I feel that certain something that I can't say exactly in words. . . . I sometimes think I could paint it in a painting—someday I plan to do that or be able to express to a painter what I feel so they can put it down in a picture for our bedroom or a very special place in our home." She notes that the next day she'll "take Skipper to mother's," and signs off, "goodnight, sweetheart, hurry home." (In another note, Mattie writes, "If Skipper doesn't keep me up tonight maybe I can lay down with you for a while"; another still features a drawing of John and Mattie kissing.)

P. 90–91

Prince in front of the family car, May 1960, just before his second birthday, with his nickname, "Skipper," scrawled in blue ink.

P. 93

Prince and Tyka, August 1961.

P. 96

John Nelson kept several photos of Mattie in his wallet. Prince came into possession of this wallet at some point after his father died in August 2001; he kept it at Paisley Park, its contents intact. It was discovered on the second floor, in a trunk full of Prince's spiral notebooks, in June 2016.

P. 99

John visits a park with Tyka and Prince, September 1962.

P. 100, TOP

An envelope addressed to "Skipper Nelson Baker"—reflecting Prince's new name—from a friend in Hempstead, NY, January 2, 1971. After John and Mattie divorced, she married Hayward Baker in 1968.

P. 100, BOTTOM

Prince, already sharing his father's keen eye for fashion, in a photo taken when he was ten or eleven.

P. 102

For thirty-five years, John worked in Honeywell Manufacturing's plastic molding department, where, according to the writer Jon Bream, he produced rheostats for furnaces. His daughter Sharon says he was Honeywell's first black employee.

P. 104–05

A flyer and business cards advertise the Prince Rogers Trio, John Nelson's jazz group. Prince kept a copy of this flyer in the vault at Paisley Park. Note that "Laura," the song Prince recalls in his memoir pages, is listed among the trio's repertoire at the top of the right column. In an undated photo, John (far right, back) presides over the group, which bears "Prince Rogers" insignia on its music stands.

P. 106–07

This ninth-grade photo of Prince appeared in the 1973 yearbook for Bryant Junior High School. His father displayed it on his piano.

P. 108

In a "4th Quarter Mid-Term Progress Report" from Bryant Junior High, Prince's teacher Mrs. Hoben writes that "Prince could be doing much better work than he is, even though it is already above average. He has fine skills and a clever, perceptive mind." This was one of a few report cards he kept in the vault at Paisley Park.

P. 110

Prince performs with his high-school band, Grand Central, in the early seventies at Minneapolis's Plymouth Community Center. His cousin Charles "Chazz" Smith is on the drums.

P. 111

"Hey, did you know that too much sex makes your hair grow?" Prince displays his precocity and sense of humor in this work from his high school years, later stored in the vault at Paisley Park.

P. 112

Prince strikes a shy pose in February 1973, when he was fourteen.

P. 113

Prince's sketch of a musician, drawn in the early seventies.

P. 115, TOP
"Puberty hit with the strength of a hurricane." Prince in his sophomore year of high school, as seen in the 1974 Central High School yearbook.

P. 115, BOTTOM
By late high school, Prince had bought "a vanilla Stratocaster identical 2 the one Jimi played at Woodstock."

P. 116
"Marcie loved inner exploration as much as ☜ did." Marcie Dixon sent photos to Prince regularly. This one is dated August 30, 1976. A note to him on the back reads, "Remember that I will always have a place in my heart for you, no matter what happens."

P. 117
"Her name was Cari." Prince recalled Cari in "Schoolyard," an unreleased song from 1990: "I was only sixteen and her name was Cari / She was the number one little girl I wanted to marry me / She was only 14, but she had the major body / Yeah, this girl was mean . . ."

P. 118
A group photo of Grand Central circa 1975. From left to right: William "Hollywood" Doughty, Prince, Linda Anderson, André Anderson, Morris Day, and Terry Jackson. (Photo: Charles Chamblis)

P. 119
In the vault, Prince kept a series of buttons from the early seventies, when he was in junior high.

Part II.
For You

P. 120
Prince stands outside shirtless in an undated Polaroid.

P. 122–36 Photo Book: June 1977–April 1978
Early in the morning of December 19, 1977, a sleepless Prince decided to put together a photo book. He was nineteen years old,

and only days away from finishing the studio sessions for his debut album, *For You*. With the end of the year approaching and the record nearing completion, he took a step back to reflect on what he'd accomplished—and to memorialize the journey that had led him to the threshold of stardom.

Since early October, Prince had been recording *For You* nearly nonstop, often late into the night, playing every instrument on every song and taking on the bulk of the production responsibilities. In his perfectionism, he'd blown through his budget for the project. And he was a long way from home: Though he'd hoped to make *For You* in Minneapolis, he ended up instead at the Record Plant in Sausalito, California, a state-of-the-art facility where some of his favorite artists, such as Santana and Fleetwood Mac, had recorded, too.

"I was a physical wreck when I finished the record," Prince would later tell *Musician* magazine. But whatever exhaustion or anxiety he felt was tempered with confidence, even exuberance, as his photo book demonstrates. He was enjoying his first taste of success. His manager, Owen Husney, had rented him a beautiful three-story house at 653 Redwood Avenue, in Corte Madera, with a view of San Francisco Bay. The two of them lived there throughout the creation of *For You,* along with Prince's best friend and musical collaborator, André "Cymone" Anderson; Husney's wife, Britt; another friend and engineer, David "Z" Rivkin, whom Prince valued for his production prowess; and the record's executive producer, Tommy Vicari. Together, the group had become a kind of surrogate family for Prince, keeping his morale up—and his stomach full—between his grueling sessions at the studio.

Prince's photo book covers these fruitful months in San Francisco, but its earliest photos date to June 1977, when he signed a three-album deal with Warner Bros. Records. He continued to update the book through April 1978, when *For You* was released. When this photo album was discovered, all the pictures had fallen out of it; we've reconstructed it as accurately as possible.

P. 123, TOP

"My first car! Cute, huh?" Enjoying the fruits of his first-ever paycheck from Warner Bros., Prince reclines on the hood of his new baby-blue 1977 Datsun 200SX in Minneapolis, July 1977.

P. 123, BOTTOM

"The talking fly and his trainer, Miss Pickupandbook." Prince's sister Tyka and his best friend, André Anderson, in Minneapolis, July 1977.

P. 124, TOP
"First car wash." The Datsun gets the royal treatment in Minneapolis, July 1977.

P. 124, CENTER
"Shut up!" In October 1977, when Prince, Husney, and the others moved to Corte Madera to begin recording *For You,* Tommy Vicari went with them. He was in the unenviable position of sleeping on the couch in their Corte Madera rental house. Prince would rouse him at all hours for marathon sessions in the studio. Vicari had years of experience in the music business, and he was quick to grasp Prince's enormous talent—but Prince was soon hoping to send him home. Vicari was often the butt of his practical jokes—as in this photo, the first of many taken immediately after Prince had shaken him awake.

P. 124, BOTTOM
"Eddie and Sancheze." André's brother Eddie Anderson in Minneapolis, June 1977.

P. 125, TOP
"I usually bring my teeth to the studio." Prince sits behind the keyboards at Sound 80, a studio in Minneapolis, September 1977. Evidently, he felt that this picture made him look like someone whose dentures had gone missing. He briefly began work on *For You* at Sound 80—and in the comfort of his hometown, where he hoped to remain—before he was forced to relocate. He'd convinced Warner Bros. that he could produce the album himself, but they'd compromised by sending Tommy Vicari, an industry veteran, to oversee the engineering of the record. Sound 80 had recently installed a new studio console—so new, in fact, that Vicari felt it would take months to work the kinks out of it. Rather than lose time, Prince and the label agreed to move production to the Record Plant, in Sausalito.

P. 125, BOTTOM
"The wind does great things for one's hair!" Prince relaxes on a sailboat in Minneapolis, July 1977.

P. 126, TOP
"View from the cell I was in when I signed my 1st record contract." In late June 1977, Prince and Husney flew out to Los Angeles to close the deal with Warner Bros. They stayed at the Sheraton Universal Hotel—about a ten-minute drive from the label's headquarters—where Prince took this photo.

P. 126, CENTER

"Pee-pee is not a bad word." André Anderson's mother, Bernadette Anderson, smiles for Prince's camera in Minneapolis, July 1977. As Prince would later write in his memoir pages, Bernadette was a major figure in his life, and a fixture in the North Minneapolis community, where she was the director of the YWCA. When Prince was in his mid-teens and on the outs with his parents, Bernadette had taken him under her wing, inviting him to live with her and her six children—of whom André was the youngest—at 1244 Russell Avenue North. With his family life finally stabilized, Prince spent a lot of time in the Andersons' basement, making music with André. They formed Grand Central with Prince's cousin Chazz Smith on drums, later replaced by Morris Day. Prince, who once said he planned to devote "a whole chapter" to Bernadette in his memoir, was still living under her roof when Husney became his manager in 1976.

P. 126, BOTTOM

"Fox strolling down a block in L.A." Los Angeles, June 1977.

P. 127, TOP

"Sunset in L.A." Los Angeles, June 1977.

P. 127, CENTER

"My first check from the company." When the Warner Bros. deal was signed at last, the label delivered Prince's first check to the Sheraton Universal Hotel. Dated June 24, 1977—less than three weeks after his nineteenth birthday—it was made out to Prince Rogers Nelson and American Artists (Husney's management company) for the amount of eighty thousand dollars, an advance on royalties. Prince was enraptured by the check, which began to translate all of his hard work and preternatural talent into material terms. He staged this photo with a pen and an afro comb nearby, as if he'd picked out his hair just before signing it.

Less thrilling was all the hobnobbing that Warner Bros. expected of him. To celebrate the signing, the label had hosted a reception at La Serre, a luxe French restaurant on Ventura Boulevard. Prince so dreaded the prospect of mingling with record execs that his friend David Rivkin suggested he record a song for the occasion; he could convey his gratitude through music without having to work the room. The result was "I Hope We Work It Out," an unreleased song about "Makin' music naturally, me and W.B." Apparently a hit among the La Serre crowd, the song found Prince seducing his new label: "Now that I know your name and you know mine / Ain't it just about time that we got together? / We could make such beautiful music . . . forever."

The song ends with a bomb going off—a prophetic hint of Prince's high-profile dispute with the label in the nineties.

P. 127, BOTTOM
"View from the Sheraton Universal Hotel." Another June 1977 photo of the city as Prince saw it when he signed his first record contract.

P. 128, TOP
" 'Hey, what's happening?' Bad Dad." John Nelson in Minneapolis, October 1977.

P. 128, CENTER
" 'Hit me in the chest! Go ahead, take your best shot!' " André Anderson in Minneapolis, October 1977.

P. 128, BOTTOM
" 'The lawn and Robin Crockett.' " Prince snapped this shot of his neighborhood friend Robin Crockett in October 1977. In 2007, Crockett bought the Anderson home on Russell Avenue, where Prince and André would rehearse. In a 2018 interview with *Vogue's* Rebecca Bengal, Crockett remembered, "We would sit on that corner there on Plymouth in our pink foam hair curlers and wait for the go-ahead so we could come over and be groupies and watch them practice. It was okay to be a groupie! It was part of our culture. We were north-siders and so were they. . . . This basement had a lot going on. This is it. This is where greatness came from."

P. 129, TOP
"(My cousin Deniece)." Minneapolis, October 1977.

P. 129, CENTER
"Tommy, in his usual position." The next phase in the rude awakening of Tommy Vicari, Corte Madera, October 1977.

P. 129, BOTTOM
"This broad could stop traffic." In June 1977, Prince snapped this shot of a Los Angeles billboard promoting Minnie Riperton's album *Stay in Love,* released that February. A few years later, a billboard for his second album, *Prince,* would appear on Sunset Boulevard. And several decades down the line, in 2011, Riperton's daughter, Maya Rudolph, would form a Prince cover band called Princess with her friend Gretchen Lieberum. In a 2015 interview with *L. A. Weekly,* the pair explained that they'd earned Prince's approval: "He gave us both these big, nice hugs, and he said that he had our performance on Jimmy Fallon recorded on his DVR."

P. 130, TOP LEFT

"Kiss me, c'mon, I dare you!" Bobby "Z." Rivkin in Minneapolis, July 1977. Later, Bobby Z. would become the drummer for The Revolution.

P. 130, TOP RIGHT

"No, this not a postcard!" Prince takes in a picturesque view of the Golden Gate Bridge, October 1977.

P. 130, BOTTOM

"I must prove to the world that blind people can play tennis, too!" Leaning against Prince's Datsun, André Anderson holds a tennis racket and squints with determination. Minneapolis, September or October 1977.

P. 131, TOP

"My first 'money-paying gig' was done here. Capacity crowd of 113 came. Boy, was it wet." Minneapolis's Bethune Park and Phillis Wheatley Community Center, July 1977.

P. 131, CENTER

"2 pages later, still there! Yes, there's sleep in your eyes!" Prince continues to torment Tommy Vicari, who is, yes, still on the couch, and still looking sleepy. Corte Madera, October 1977.

P. 131, BOTTOM

"Pwince!" By June 1977, Prince was still close with Marcie Dixon. Nearly forty years later, in his memoir pages, he would write that she was the only one who understood how he felt about music.

P. 132

"BEFORE . . . and after the operation." During a car ride, Prince gives himself the Groucho Marx treatment, with astonishing results. Minneapolis, July 1977.

P. 133, TOP

"My First House." In April 1978, the same month that *For You* came out, Prince put some of his Warner Bros. advance toward a home at 5215 France Avenue S, near Edina, a suburb of Minneapolis. In the basement he assembled a rudimentary home studio, his first, allowing him to record whatever he wanted, whenever he wanted—a practice he'd continue as he moved into successive homes around the Minneapolis area, culminating in the creation of Paisley Park about a decade later.

P. 133, CENTER
"Now's as good a time as any to learn to ride this mug." Prince's father, John Nelson, then sixty-one, bikes around Minneapolis, April 1978.

P. 133, BOTTOM
"Sausalito." In October 1977, as Prince approached the studio where he'd spend the next months recording and perfecting his first album, he indulged his inner tourist, taking this photo of the glimmering waterfront.

P. 134, TOP
"View from front yard at house in L.A." In January 1978, with initial tracking on *For You* complete, Prince and his companions decamped to Los Angeles to mix the record at a different studio, Sound Labs. Owen Husney rented another furnished house for the group at 2810 Montcalm Avenue, in the Hollywood Hills.

P. 134, BOTTOM
"Venice, Californy. Pictured with cane is Thomas Edison." Prince takes in the passersby—young, old, and ancient—at Venice Beach, January 1978.

P. 135, TOP AND CENTER
"I got five hits!" and "Why don'tcha come up and see me and the dog sometimes." Pepé Willie, shown here in Minneapolis in April 1978, had become a kind of mentor to Prince, who was twelve when they first met. The husband of Prince's cousin Shauntel Manderville, Willie was a musician, too, and in 1975 he tapped Prince to record with his band, 94 East, giving the sixteen-year-old his first exposure to the studio. "Prince played better than a professional session player, and I've been to a lot of sessions," Willie told *Rolling Stone* in 2016. "None of the guitar players I'd worked with played as well as Prince for his first time in a recording studio. It just totally blew my mind."

P. 135, BOTTOM
"The bumproom in L.A." January 1978.

P. 136, CENTER
"Don't worry! I've seen better faces on an Iodine bottle!" Prince in Minneapolis, July 1977.

P. 136, BOTTOM
"2810 Montcalm, André in window, Tommy & Diane is right dare." Los Angeles, January 1978.

P. 137–203
Prince's words in this section and the next are drawn from the following sources: Jon Bream, "Our Teenage Virtuoso Is Home To Play at Last," *The Minneapolis Star,* January 5, 1979; Bream, "World of Music Gets a Sexy Prince," *The Minneapolis Star,* February, 1980; Tim Carr, "Prince: A One-Man Band and a Whole Chorus, Too," *The Minneapolis Tribune,* April 30, 1978; Barbara Graustark, "Prince: Strange Tales from Andre's Basement," *Musician,* September 1983; Robert Hilburn, "The Renegade Prince," *Los Angeles Times,* November 21, 1982; Cynthia Horner, "A Close Encounter with Prince!," *Right On!,* January 1979; Larry King interview, *Larry King Live,* December 10, 1999; Lynn Normant, "Ebony Interview with Prince," *Ebony,* July 1986; Jeff Schneider, "Prince," *Insider,* May/June 1978; Andy Schwartz, "Prince: A Dirty Mind Comes Clean," *New York Rocker,* June 1981; and Steve Sutherland, "Someday Your Prince Will Come," *Melody Maker,* June 1981.

P. 138–41
While he was staying at the house on Montcalm Avenue in January 1978, Prince wrote captions on the backs of several photographs, apparently intending to mail them to someone. At the time of his death, they were in the vault at Paisley Park.

P. 142–43
Prince plays a guitar in bed at his new home on France Avenue, April 1978. (Photo © 1986 Joseph Gianetti)

P. 144–46
"I took this picture of the heater and I, in the bathroom mirror," Prince wrote. This turned out to be part of a more extensive photo shoot he'd undertaken alone in the bathroom at 2810 Montcalm, wearing red leggings, cutoff jeans, and, occasionally, a fake hand. ("If you understand my color, put your hand in your crotch," he would later sing on "Purple Music.")

P. 147
Prince in Minneapolis, April 1978, when his debut album, *For You,* was released.

P. 148–49
Prince standing before the hills of the Bay Area, October 1977.

P. 151

Though he didn't include it in his photo book, Prince held on to this snapshot from an earlier trip to Los Angeles, taken on May 27, 1977. Before he'd signed with Warner Bros., he'd been courted by A&M Records, who flew him out and put him up at the Beverly Wilshire Hotel. He posed on the hotel's red-carpeted steps and wrote "On A&M" on the back of the photo.

P. 152

During the final days of tracking on *For You*—and, coincidentally, at the same time he was beginning to put together this photo book—Prince broke his treasured Polymoog synthesizer, one of the instruments that he felt would give him a new and distinctive sound. Husney rushed out to rent another one from Shirley Walker, a film composer. "Good luck with the album," she wrote on the invoice. "Hope it goes platinum in the 1st week."

P. 153

Another shot of Prince at work in the studio at Sound 80 in Minneapolis, making demos of the songs from *For You,* September 1977.

P. 154–56

These two versions of the lyrics to "Soft and Wet," Prince's first single, find him establishing creative patterns he'd maintain throughout his career. First, the production of multiple handwritten drafts of his lyrics, each one a refinement of the last; second, the use of playful pseudonyms to distance himself from his work. Here, he uses "Percy," a name he'd return to throughout the seventies, sometimes in conjunction with "Bagonia." Another notebook saw him list such false names as "Dexter Cunningbowl," "Alfred Horkelsby," "Seymou," and "Harriet Tubman."

Prince wrote "Soft and Wet" no later than the summer of 1976. He cowrote the lyrics with Chris Moon, the founder of Moon Sound, an eight-track studio in South Minneapolis where Prince recorded much of his earliest work. Warner Bros. released the finished single, taken from *For You,* on June 7, 1978, Prince's twentieth birthday. It reached #92 on Billboard's Hot 100 chart, and #12 on their Hot Soul Singles chart.

P. 157–58

As his debut album went from fantasy to reality, Prince took pleasure in imagining and sketching every facet of the record, from the cover art to the promotional credits to the track list, the last of which was ever evolving. Only three songs listed here ("For You," "Soft and Wet," and "Baby") made it onto the final record. Another iteration of the *For You* track listing includes "Sometimes It Snows in April," a song that would reappear on his 1986 album *Parade*.

P. 159
Producing his own work, Prince was meticulous about his vocal harmonies, overdubbing dozens of versions of himself hitting different notes to generate the rich chords he wanted. To keep all of his harmonies straight, he would make a careful list of the parts of the song and the different notes he needed to hit, as he did here, for "Baby."

P. 160
Prince kept his sense of humor during long hours in the studio, as demonstrated by this worksheet he kept to track the levels of various tracks and faders while mixing "Baby." It includes references to Chaka Khan, Bianca Jagger, Joni Mitchell, and Tommy Vicari, plus a doodle of two people kissing—reminiscent, in a way, of the drawings his mother used to make for his father.

P. 161
A doodle Prince made in his notebook of *For You* lyrics, circa 1976–77. The notebook also includes an early draft of "Sometimes It Snows in April," a song Prince wouldn't release for another decade.

P. 162
Prince as glimpsed in the rearview mirror of his new Datsun, July 1977.

P. 163
Outtakes from Joseph Giannetti's *For You* photo shoot at a Macy's in San Francisco, 1977. (Photos © 1986 Joseph Giannetti)

P. 164–65
To support the "Soft and Wet" single, Prince embarked on a signing tour, appearing at record stores throughout the country to give his autograph to his new fans. These were supposed to be intimate promotional events—instead, Prince found himself engulfed in crowds even younger than he was. He's shown here at the Record Factory in Oakland, California; at another signing, fans overwhelmed him with his poster.

P. 166
Prince strikes a defiant pose in this outtake from the *Dirty Mind* cover shoot, circa 1980. (Photography © 1985 Allen Beaulieu)

Part III.
Controversy

P. 168–69

In 1979, Warner Bros. mounted a billboard on Sunset Boulevard to support *Prince.* Its single "I Wanna Be Your Lover" proved to be Prince's most successful song yet, making #11 on the Billboard Hot 100 and #1 on the Billboard Hot Soul Singles chart. Warner Bros.' media information packet boasted, "From his outrageous costuming, or lack of costuming, to his sensual, suggestive lyrics and scintillating rock/disco/R&B fusion, Prince is as flamboyant as any music star has a right to be."

P. 170–71

As with *For You,* Prince had a clear idea for the cover of his self-titled follow-up: He presented himself shirtless with a solemn expression against a blue background. Outtakes from the October 1979 session show him finding the right mix of distance and intimacy to preserve his mystique. (Photos © Jurgen Reisch for Warner Bros.)

P. 172–73

Prince took an active role in Warner Bros.' marketing and promotion of his work, never wanting the label to pigeonhole him. He held on to many of the production proofs and press kits from his early career, such as this set of guidelines for the promotional posters for his second album, 1979's *Prince.* (Proof © Warner Bros. Photo of Prince © Jurgen Reisch)

P. 174

Wearing the provocative trench coat and bikini outfit that became an early trademark, Prince shaves in his dressing room before a date on the tour for *Dirty Mind,* his third record. The tour ran from December 1980 to April 1981. (Photography © 1985 Allen Beaulieu)

P. 175–78

Allen Beaulieu photographed Prince and his band for the 1980 *Dirty Mind* album; these are some of the outtakes, with a few featuring Prince's guitarist Dez Dickerson. Prince told Beaulieu that he wanted to appear on a bed on the album cover. It was

Beaulieu's idea to buy a worn-out box spring from a junkyard and photograph Prince in front of the springs. (Photography © 1985 Allen Beaulieu)

P. 179
Prince strips down to bikini briefs during a performance on the *Dirty Mind* tour at Sam's in Minneapolis, on March 9, 1981. (Photography © 1985 Allen Beaulieu)

P. 180–81
A close-up of Prince from the early eighties. (Photography © 1985 Allen Beaulieu)

P. 182–83
Prince's handwritten lyrics for "Dirty Mind," the title track from his third album, seem to suggest that he was entertaining the title "Naughty Mind" at first. His keyboardist, Matt "Doctor" Fink, remembered cowriting the song with him. "It germinated in the midst of a rehearsal jam session," he told Matthew Wilkening of *Diffuser* in 2017. "We would always warm up before working on songs for a new record. Just off the top of my head during one of those jams, I started that chord progression. . . . At the end of rehearsal that day he said, 'I want you to come to the house tonight'—he had a studio set up in his house at that time—'I want to work on that jam you did.'" By the next morning, Prince had "a finished demo version with full vocals and lyrics and guitars on it and everything all done. He says, 'Have a listen to this guys, I think this is gonna be the title track to the third album.'" Recording for the album had started sometime in May or June 1980 in his latest home studio, at 680 North Arm Drive in Orono, Minnesota. The home was near Lake Minnetonka, which would appear a few years later in one of Prince's most enduring lines from the *Purple Rain* film: "You have to purify yourself in the waters of Lake Minnetonka."

P. 184–85
Four undated Polaroids from the early eighties.

P. 186–87
Prince taking a phone call in bed, circa 1980-81. (Photography © 1985 Allen Beaulieu)

P. 188–89
Prince smirks beside a pinball machine backstage during the *Controversy* tour. (Photography © 1985 Allen Beaulieu)

P. 190

Again making use of whatever was around him, Prince scrawled the lyrics to "Do Me, Baby" on a paper bag. The song made its way onto his fourth album, *Controversy,* released in 1981.

P. 191

Dirty Mind featured songs about incest and oral sex, but Prince wanted to outdo himself in his quest to shock—so he wrote "Vagina," an unreleased song from 1981 or 1982 about a lover who's "half-boy, half-girl, the best of both worlds." Putting the lyrics to paper, he chose red ink, as he'd done for much of the material on *Dirty Mind,* and he included a drawing of Vagina for good measure. It's likely that he intended the i in "Vagina" to be pronounced as a long *e,* as in the name "Gina." He'd hoped that Denise Matthews would use that name, and that pronunciation, for her stage persona; she opted instead for the tamer Vanity.

P. 193

When inspiration struck, Prince would write on whatever was handy—in this case, for "Partyup," a twelve-inch album sleeve, first in pencil, and then in thick, bright red ink, as he did for several songs on *Dirty Mind,* as if embedding his lurid intentions in the paper itself. The album artwork contained many images of dripping red spray paint—a continuation of this aesthetic. Writing quickly, Prince would revise his lyrics on the fly. The published lyrics to "Do It All Night," for instance, omitted some lewd words visible in Prince's handwritten version: "I drown, baby, drown, baby, in your arms" was originally "I'll make you drown, baby, drown, baby, in your come." Radio DJs received copies of *Dirty Mind* with a warning sticker: *Programmers: Please audition before airing.*

P. 194–95

Prince sips some orange juice backstage during the *Dirty Mind* tour, 1981. (Photography © 1985 Allen Beaulieu)

P. 196–97

A Polaroid of the collage designed by Prince for the preliminary cover of his fifth album, *1999,* released in 1982.

P. 199

This early draft of "1999" is full of cross-outs and markups. Most notably, it reveals that the first line was originally, "I was trippin' when I wrote this."

P. 200

Morris Day, the front man for the Time, exchanges high fives with the elusive "Jamie Starr" in these two photos from the early eighties. Starr and "The Starr * Company" received production credit on the Time's first two albums, as well as Vanity 6's album and *Dirty Mind,* among others. In 1982, Prince made a point of telling the *Los Angeles Times:* "I'm not Jamie Starr." In fact, he was Jamie Starr. "I was just getting tired of seeing my name," he told *Bass Player* in 1999. "If you give away an idea, you still own that idea. In fact, giving it away strengthens it. Why do people feel they have to take credit for everything they do? Ego—that's the only reason." To further the Starr illusion, Prince had Allen Beaulieu shoot him dressed incognito as Jamie Starr in the studio with Morris Day. Prince's hair was whitened, a bra was slung over his chair, a girlie magazine was splayed open on the studio console, a full ashtray was set beside him, and dollar bills were scattered around. The Heinz bottle near the faders is probably chili sauce, the Time's signature condiment. Whenever someone in the group called out "chili sauce!" the band would know to change its groove. Prince and the Time were so fond of the phrase that it became the title of a song on the Time's 1984 album, *Ice Cream Castle*. (Photography © 1985 Allen Beaulieu)

P. 201

The vinyl pressing of *1999* featured a photograph of Prince's left eye on its label; as the record spins, the eye swirls around hypnotically. He retained a copy of the proof from Warner Bros.

P. 202

Prince refused to explain the meaning of his lyrics or the circumstances behind them. "They are yours to make what you want of them," he told the London *Times* in 1996. "I don't want to spoil the process by explaining what I think they are about." Speaking to *Musician* in September 1983, he said of "Little Red Corvette," "That song was a real-life incident. A girl in a little red Corvette . . ." But he didn't elaborate, and he may have been feinting.

Like much of *1999*, on which it appears, "Little Red Corvette" was tracked at Prince's home studio at 9401 Kiowa Trail, in Chanhassen, Minnesota. The song was his first top-ten hit in the United States. After he wrote this iteration of the lyrics, Prince decided to change "try to wreck your little red love machine" to "tame your little red love machine." There's also an additional couplet at the end, a variant of which ended up in the song's rare "dance mix": "Cush, cush, cushion in a velvet sweat, / Suck it all night so you don't forget! Mayday!"

Part IV.
Baby I'm a Star

P. 204
Prince held on to dozens of continuity Polaroids taken during the filming of *Purple Rain,* where the crew had to be sure to keep his appearance consistent between takes.

P. 206–16
This is an eleven-page handwritten treatment for the film that evolved into *Purple Rain.* Prince may have written these pages as early as the spring or summer of 1982. Since that March, if not earlier, he'd been thinking about making a movie based on his life; he'd proposed embellishing *The Second Coming,* a concert film of the *Controversy* tour directed by Chuck Statler, with dramatic autobiographical interludes. Though he soon halted work on the concert movie, which remains unreleased, he remained attached to the idea of a feature film—something that borrowed from his vexed connection to his parents, their divorce, and the tight-knit music scene in Minneapolis, with its rivalries and fierce ambitions.

These pages seem to have been Prince's first attempt to work out the film's plot. They see him ruminating on the same themes that animated *Purple Rain* and, decades later, his memoir pages. His management company hired William Blinn, a teleplay writer who'd worked on *Roots,* to put together a script. Blinn delivered a draft called *Dreams* in May 1983 and a revision that July, but he had to begin another job before the film found a director.

Soon after Albert Magnoli came onboard, Prince parted ways with Vanity, whom he'd always envisioned as his love interest in the film. She was replaced by Apollonia Kotero. The movie had a new title, too: *Purple Rain,* after a song Prince had written that summer and performed live for the first time on August 3, at First Avenue.

Magnoli rewrote the script, losing some of the darker elements that had been in Prince's treatment and Blinn's drafts. Still, it's surprising how much of the film reflects what Prince envisioned in these early notes.

Purple Rain began principal photography in November 1983 and was released in July 1984. Its soundtrack album includes only two of the eight songs he considered for the film in this writing: "Baby I'm a Star" and "I Would Die 4 U."

P. 222–50

Prince's words in this section are drawn from the following sources: Susie Boon, "The Artist Informally," *Top of the Pops,* May 1997; Jon Bream, "Our Teenage Virtuoso Is Home to Play at Last," *The Minneapolis Star,* January 5, 1979; Cheo Hodari Coker, "A Night with Prince," *Essence,* June 2014; Robert L. Doerschuk, "The Sound of Emancipation," *Musician,* April 1997; Steve Fargnoli with Prince, "MTV Presents Prince," MTV, November 13, 1985; Neil Karlen, "Prince Talks: The Silence Is Broken," *Rolling Stone,* September 12, 1985; Lynn Normant, "*Ebony* Interview with Prince," *Ebony,* July 1986; Chris Rock interview with Prince, *VH1 to One,* January 1997; and Prince's debut Piano & A Microphone performance at Paisley Park, January 21, 2016.

P. 222–23

Prince may have written "Let's Go Crazy" as early as 1982; the first demo version came in May 1983 at his home studio in Chanhassen. The version on *Purple Rain* was recorded live that August 7, with the Revolution, in the warehouse where the band rehearsed. This handwritten version adds another foreboding line to the preacherly monologue that opens the song: "So u better try to be happy 'cause one day the sun may set for good."

P. 224–25

This draft of the "Computer Blue" lyrics is mottled with a mysterious purple liquid, and Prince has written the word "Purple" on the back with an elegant cursive flourish. He wrote many lines that didn't make into the recorded song, including a dismissal of "icky cellophane love affairs." When Prince and the Revolution recorded "Computer Blue" in August 1983, it stretched to more than fourteen minutes, including a brooding speech in which Prince named various hallways in his home after emotions: lust, fear, insecurity, hate, pain. Prince instructed his bandmates Wendy Melvoin and Lisa Coleman to begin the song by reciting a short conversation he'd written: "Wendy?" "Yes, Lisa." "Is the water warm enough?" "Yes, Lisa." "Shall we begin?" "Yes, Lisa." He may have had in mind a lyric from his handwritten version: "You say you want a relationship based on give and take. Tell u what: I'll give you a baby if u take a bath."

P. 226

When Tipper Gore heard her daughter listening to "Darling Nikki" in 1984, she was so unsettled by Prince's talk of masturbation that she founded the Parents Music Resource Center, a committee that inspired the record industry to slap Parental

Advisory stickers on albums with "explicit lyrics." She wrote in her 1987 book *Raising PG Kids in an X-Rated Society,* "I couldn't believe my ears! The vulgar lyrics embarrassed both of us. At first, I was stunned—then I got mad!" Presumably the additional verse to "Darling Nikki" seen here—"Twice she cooked me dinner / Taste like shit both times"—would not have improved Gore's enthusiasm for the song, which Prince recorded in July 1983 at his Kiowa Trail home studio in Chanhassen. He would reference Tipper Gore occasionally throughout his career. At a 2001 press conference announcing the first Celebration at Paisley Park, he explained that the event would be family friendly because he'd renounced profanity. "Even Tipper Gore can come," he said.

P. 227–29

"I don't want money. I don't want love. If I wanted either one, I would buy it. I want the heavy stuff. What your dreams are made of. I want control. I've got the keys, now gimme the driver's seat. Try it." In an early draft of "Purple Rain," Prince experiments with the lovelorn, inspirational tone that made this his most famous song. He was writing in a self-consciously epic mode, delivering a rock-ballad sound in an effort to reach a broader audience. "Trust me," he writes, "I'm not a politician, I'm a purple musician, and I only want to set u free." (Similarly, in set lists for his 2016 Piano & A Microphone tour, he would refer to his song "Purple Music" as "Welcome 2 the Freedom Galaxy.")

P. 231

A photo of Prince and his longtime bodyguard, "Big Chick" Huntsberry, standing outside Prince's purple house on Kiowa Trail in the mid-eighties. At the time of his death, Prince kept this framed photograph in his dressing room on the second floor of Paisley Park.

P. 232

This early version of "Raspberry Beret," a song Prince first recorded at Los Angeles's Sunset Sound in 1982, contains several verses that didn't end up in the cut of the song released on 1985's *Around the World in a Day.* The lines in which the narrator awakes to find that his lover has gone away and left "a note on the floor" anticipate "Darling Nikki," which he'd record more than a year later.

Albert Magnoli's *Purple Rain* script included a scene in which Prince and Vanity make love in a barn during a thunderstorm. Some iteration of this scene was filmed, but it was edited out of the finished movie. It may have been on Prince's mind in September 1984, when he recorded the final version of "Raspberry Beret" with some new lyrics: "The rain sounds so cool when it hits the barn roof / And the horses wonder who you are / Thunder drowns out what the lightning sees / You feel like a movie star."

P. 235
Prince recorded "Kiss"—called "Your Kiss" in this handwritten draft—on April 28, 1985, at Sunset Sound in Los Angeles. He intended to give the song to Mazarati, a band helmed by his longtime friend David "Z" Rivkin and the Revolution's bassist, Brown Mark; they were working at Sunset Sound at the time, too. After Prince gave them a demo of the song, he was so impressed by their reworking of it that he insisted on having it back—they'd turned it into something funky. The next night, using their version as a foundation, he produced the version released on *Parade* the following year, which reached #1 on the Billboard Hot 100 chart.

P. 237–38
Jeff Katz took Prince's photo for the 1986 *Parade* cover, out-takes of which are seen here. When Prince had to renew his passport a few months after the album came out, he used one of Katz's pictures. (Photos: Jeff Katz)

P. 240–45
In February 1986, Rebecca Blake directed the music video for "Kiss," in which a woman in a veil and sunglasses dances with Prince while Wendy Melvoin strums the guitar. Blake sent story-boards of the concept for Prince's approval. "I was very determined that it not look like a music video, whatever that meant at the time, and that it would just sort of have this very pared-down discipline," she told *The Golden Age of Music Video*. "I did it in a kind of very minimal way, purposely." (Storyboard © Warner Bros.)

P. 246–47
Prince and his father—both sporting ruffled sleeves—are pictured here during the *Purple Rain* era, likely at the 1985 American Music Awards. According to one friend, Prince wanted his memoir to reclaim the narrative about his father, whom he feared too many people conflated with the father character in the *Purple Rain* film.

P. 248–49
Prince wrote these lyrics for "The Beautiful Ones" with some urgency on the backside of a work order from Sunset Sound, the Los Angeles studio where he recorded the bulk of *Purple*

Rain. As Duane Tudahl describes in *Prince and the Purple Rain Era Studio Sessions,* "The Beautiful Ones" came together on September 20, 1983, over the course of a single session lasting nearly seventeen hours, with Prince performing every part himself. As he often did, he asked the studio engineers to step outside while he recorded his vocal takes; these lyrics suggest that he noted the chords to give himself vocal cues, changing a few lyrics on the fly and editing others out later. According to Prince's engineer Susan Rogers, he'd likely written the music about two months earlier, during the summer. He refused to say who the song was about, and his sense that it was often misinterpreted may have been part of what inspired him to begin the memoir named after it. We'll never know for certain.

P. 250–51
Prince, resplendent in the spotlight during the *Purple Rain* tour in 1984. (Photo: Nancy Bundt)

Acknowledgments

This book would not have been possible without the help and support of Angela Aycock, Meron Bekure, Andrea Bruce, Troy Carter, Mengfei Chen, Nicole Counts, John DeLaney, Phaedra Ellis-Lamkins, Richard Elman, Cecil Flores, Julie Grau, Trevor Guy, Rebecca Holzman, Michael Howe, Chris Jackson, Kirk Johnson, London King, Dan Kirschen, Matthew Martin, Alex Mitchell, Tyka and President Nelson, Esther Newberg, Loren Noveck, Vicky Osterweil, Patricia and Julie Piepenbring, Jennifer Raczak, Bobby "Z" Rivkin, David "Z" Rivkin, Rachel Rokicki, P. J. Scott, Natasha Stagg, Duane Tudahl, Laura Van der Veer, Hayden VanEarden, Andrianna Yeatts, Homa Zarghamee, and Peter Bravestrong.

Credits

Pages 188–89, Prince in front of a pinball machine: Photography © 1985 Allen Beaulieu

Page 190, "Do Me, Baby": Words and Music by Prince Rogers Nelson © Universal Music Works on behalf of NPG Music Publishing, LLC (GMR)

Page 191, "Vagina": Words and Music by Prince Rogers Nelson © Universal Music Works on behalf of NPG Music Publishing, LLC (GMR)

Page 193, "Party Up": Words and Music by Prince Rogers Nelson © Universal Music Works on behalf of NPG Music Publishing, LLC (GMR)

Pages 194–95, Prince drinking out of a paper cup: Photography © 1985 Allen Beaulieu

Pages 196–97, album art: © The Prince Estate

Page 199, "1999". Words and Music by Prince Rogers Nelson © Universal Music Works on behalf of NPG Music Publishing, LLC (GMR)

Page 200, "Jamie Starr" with Morris Day: Photography © 1985 Allen Beaulieu

Page 201: © Warner Bros.

Page 202, "Little Red Corvette": Words and Music by Prince Rogers Nelson © Universal Music Works on behalf of NPG Music Publishing, LLC (GMR)

Pages 206–15, handwritten synopsis of Purple Rain: © The Prince Estate

Page 216, song list: © The Prince Estate

Pages 222–23, "Let's Go Crazy": Words and Music by Prince Rogers Nelson © Universal Music Works on behalf of NPG Music Publishing, LLC (GMR)

Pages 224–25, "Computer Blue": Words and Music by Lisa Coleman, Matthew Robert Fink, Wendy Melvoin, John L. Nelson, Prince Rogers Nelson © Universal Music Works on behalf of Warner Grandview Music, and NPG Music Publishing, LLC (GMR) / Universal Music Corp. On behalf of Warner Olive Music LLC., and Controversy Music (ASCAP)

Page 226, "Darling Nikki": Words and Music by Prince Rogers Nelson © Universal Music Works on behalf of NPG Music Publishing, LLC (GMR)

Pages 227–29, "Purple Rain": Words and Music by Prince Rogers Nelson © Universal Music Works on behalf of NPG Music Publishing, LLC (GMR)

Page 232, "Raspberry Beret": Words and Music by Prince Rogers Nelson © Universal Music Works on behalf of NPG Music Publishing, LLC (GMR)

Page 235, "Kiss": Words and Music by Prince Rogers Nelson © Universal Music Works on behalf of NPG Music Publishing, LLC (GMR)

Page 237, outtakes from the Parade cover shoot, photographed by Jeff Katz: © The Prince Estate

Page 238, Prince's passport: © The Prince Estate

Pages 240–45, "Kiss" video storyboard: © Warner Bros.

Pages 248–49, "The Beautiful Ones": Words and Music by Prince Rogers Nelson © Universal Music Works on behalf of NPG Music Publishing, LLC (GMR)

Pages 250–51, Prince onstage, photographed by Nancy Bundt: © The Prince Estate

About the Authors

PRINCE ROGERS NELSON remains one of the most popular and influential musical acts of all time. Known for his style and range, Prince's prolific music career included an ever-evolving sound that blended pop, R&B, hip-hop, jazz, and soul. Prince sold more than 100 million albums worldwide, making him one of the bestselling artists of all time. He won seven GRAMMY® Awards, a Golden Globe Award, and an Academy Award® for the film *Purple Rain*. He was inducted into the Rock and Roll Hall of Fame in 2004, the first year of his eligibility. Prince tragically passed away at his Paisley Park home on April 21, 2016. His legacy lives on through the timeless messages of love in his music and the countless ways his work has touched lives.

DAN PIEPENBRING is an advisory editor at *The Paris Review* and the coauthor, with Tom O'Neill, of *Chaos: Charles Manson, the CIA, and the Secret History of the Sixties.*

31901065267553